Disgust

Lorette C. Luzajic

The author would like to acknowledge funding support from the Ontario Arts Council and the Government of Ontario for their support.

for Moshy, who is everything

He walked out in the gray light and stood and he saw for a brief moment the absolute truth of the world. The cold relentless circling of the intestate earth. Darkness implacable. The blind dogs of the sun in their running. The crushing black vacuum of the universe. And somewhere two hunted animals trembling like ground-foxes in their cover. Borrowed time and borrowed world and borrowed eyes with which to sorrow it.

Cormac McCarthy, *The Road*

Table of Contents

Winter Light

after *Adoration of the Shepherds,* by Philippe de Champaigne (France) 1640s

Even Sunday, the city is a frenzy. All scowl and growl, eyes cast low. January's slush and freeze fresh, slick and slippery. The banshee winds spooking shrill through skyrise corridors. Still, you are standing. Still here to count the day a blessing. This time last year, it was possible, likely even, that you would die.

Still fragile, you watch carefully for ice patches in the parking lot of St. Seraphim of Sarov Orthodox cathedral. The church is half empty but your heart is full of mystery as prayer fills the room. The Christmas trees and poinsettia remind you of the reason. On every wall, icon paintings of saints and intricate vines, dusty pinks and rusty reds. Ancient symbols and acronyms like ciphers. A cloud of warm frankincense. The rites here are as indecipherable to you as the Cyrillic on vellum, an unfamiliar choreography.

It is the dancing light from bouquets of beeswax candles, slender stalks bundled at either side of the altar. It is magical how it flickers against the gold leaf of Mary's halo: *Theotokos,* and the elaborate inlaid gold framing the icons that are doors between the narthex and the nave. There was a time when you were outraged by such ornaments, when some people went hungry. But today you think about the woman washing Christ's feet with rare perfumes. *The poor you will always have with you, but you will not always have*

Me. Gold is a gift, like life, and beauty is profound and rare. A taste of heaven. In this space, it belongs to everyone. The whole city can step inside to pray and partake of it. This gift of life.

You do not know these traditions, how gold symbolizes purity, the unperishable, the precious, or that it reflects the eternal light, but you feel something about it in its glow. The lowly manger, the splendour of glory, two different aspects of the same winter light.

The Divine Liturgy: men in white and gold cloaks and crosses, with candle sticks, dikirion and trikirion, glowing the unwaning light of God. Their ecstatic, mournful incantations meld with myrrh and balsam, rich and sweet as angels in the honeyed air.

Fiddleheads

after *Appalachian Mountain Sharecroppers,* by Samuel Lancaster Gerry (USA) 1870

Every morning, at dawn's first flicker in the near dark, the small girl watched the thin man descend the steep and stony incline of the hill. He filled his flask with water from the spring, drank deeply, and tipped it over his face, then filled it again. She didn't know if he saw her there all those years, or if he thought he was alone.

The thin man's bones jutted pointedly through the grungy dungarees, and his skin was as pale and moldy as cheese. Even in the grim gray shroud of morning she could see his teeth were rickety and jagged. She followed him back up the hill as far as she could from her curtained window perch. The wooden way his feet splayed to either side as he climbed reminded her of stick insects, or a daddy longlegs spider.

At the other end of the day, when the stars started rushing through the slate dark sky, she opened the screen to let the night in. If the world was still enough or the winds were blowing right, they brought down sounds of bluegrass from the steep. She fell into dreams at the medley of the fiddle, and his mournful falsetto, as beautiful as any bird soaring inland from the distant sea.

Once she had shared her heart for the hermit, an error she wouldn't make twice. After a moving message on the Beatitudes one Sunday sermon, she'd knelt in the humid alcove at the back of the chapel and pressed a few meagre coins into the prayer box. Solemnly put flame to wick and lit a candle for the thin man's soul. Why that was nice, said Mother, and the small girl opened to that rare warmth and blurted out that her prayer was for the hermit on the hill.

The girl knew from the stories all around how that no one had spoken to the thin man in her lifetime. This was the most heartbreaking thing she knew, cutting even deeper than the still small grave in the garden, the sick sister she'd come after. It made her even more sad than the Blessed Mary cradling her grown gone boy across her lap.

For goodness sakes, child, Mother huffed, save your pennies. The man on the hill does not want your piety. But the girl knew different. She heard his midnight hymns, felt them cutting her open the way his scrawny leg bones edged against their denim.

She didn't say so. Her pity, or was it love, had escaped her natural guard, and it wouldn't happen again.

One afternoon, the small girl found herself deep in the hollow, having chased after a rascally baby goat in vain. She lost her way, although her only distress was for the lost creature. She knew eventually the smoke from dinner's hearth would lead her in the direction of home. She paused when she came on a brook, cupped her hands to quench her thirst, then turned, knowing it was the same spring that she could simply follow home upstream.

When she raised herself from the cool water, she saw the thin man in the clearing, walking toward her in a misty mirage, his arms around the baby goat like the good shepherd's, and the goat bleating with such calm comfort as a purring cat.

The man set the baby goat down and broke into a wide grin when he saw how it ran toward her. His one eye was like a milk glass marble, and his ribs and clavicle were concave hollows. Thank you, Mister, she spoke, nodding and smiling, scooping low to greet the prodigal goat. The man watched her kissing her little friend and she watched him back.

I am Greta, she said finally, holding the critter skillfully in one arm and extending the hand of the other. He shrunk back into the mist. It's okay, she said, and then said it again. She felt something like courage inside her, a solid certainty at her core. I am Greta, she said again. And then, more: I am like you, because I also love music.

He stood stricken, grin turned to grimace, all those awkward bones with nowhere to hide. Tears sprang into the sockets of his face. He squeezed his eyes shut, shook his bony head from side to side, and the drops scattered into the darkening loam around them.

The small girl nodded, kept holding out one hand, but she did not threaten him by moving towards him. The few sweltering curls he had left were ash white and sticky against his scalp. She had the same ringlets he did, but hers were fiery and silk. He was as jittery as the power towers they passed once or twice a year on those rare trips into town. She could feel his nerves humming at the same speed.

After a long quiet, the wild man dashed awkwardly toward her in a moment. She wasn't frightened at all. She nodded again to assure him, to welcome him, to invite him into her circle. He raised his skinny paw, and again he looked like Christ in all those paintings, wan and wounded and wise, elongated fingertips tipped almost elegantly into a mudra. The goat was still purring. The man's hand stole fleetingly through the curls in her hair. A wail rose out of him, something born of both wonder and pain, and he drew back then, far, far back into the trees.

The small girl waved after the thin man. It's okay, she called again, even knowing he was not coming back again, even knowing she would not see him again where he would see her too. She thanked him for bringing Bella back to her, then turned homeward, filling her smock with fiddleheads in the falling light along the way.

Choked Up

after *Still Life with Oranges,* by Paul Gauguin (France) 1881

The ringing never stopped. All day, every day, one thing after another. On a good day, Nels found a certain comfort in the consistency of all the things that could go wrong with the body. Coughs, spasms, torn tendons, toothaches. It drove home our fragile common humanity, how united and connected everyone was. It didn't matter who you were or what lofty aspirations you had or didn't have, or where you came from…it all came down to the same stuff, sinews, epidermis, follicles, capillaries.

Nels usually enjoyed the constant clicking sound of the keyboard as he fielded time slots and searched for pharmacy fax numbers. His admin role was not glamourous, but it was important in its own small way. He was a cheerful secretary and liked the soothing banter he could offer as he marked in referrals and requisitions for people in need.

But today, he found himself irritable and distracted, unable to concentrate on calls and Excel cells. His mind was on yesterday's events. First, he and Sebastian had taken Minnie to the vet after a week of coughing spells. Expecting a basic kitty cold and a few pills to solve the matter, he had been surprised to find out that the wee girl had asthma. X-rays had shown scars already hardening her bronchia. Nels found himself unexpectedly sensitive about the cat's distress, imagined her struggling to breathe when he wasn't home to help her with her new feline inhaler.

And then things took another strange turn. Sebastian had cut up some orange segments to go with a nice pot of tea. When he tried to swallow the wedge, he started choking. It felt like the coughing went on and on. Tears were streaming down his face. Nels was terrified. He had no idea how to perform the Heimlich maneuver, and couldn't remember if back thumping was the first protocol or if it caused more harm. Calling 911 would be useless- these days it took an hour for services to arrive, even if someone had a gun to your head. By the time they arrived, Sebastian would be dead. Helpless, he watched Seb sputter and gasp. He was screaming inside the whole while.

He had never loved anyone the way he loved Sebastian. He'd grown his whole life around him because he felt completed in the relationship. Seb was beautiful, but he was kind and quirky and smart. They brought out the best in each other and made each laugh all the time.

Things finally settled down. But Sebastian still felt something, as if the orange was still stuck in his esophagus. Nels wondered if it could be lodged in his windpipe. Even though Seb assured him he could breathe just fine, Nels wondered if the trachea might grow inflamed and narrow the air passageway. What if the pith that was lodged there loosened, only to make him choke while he was sleeping? Nels couldn't sleep. He kept checking to see if his loved ones were breathing, Sebastian on his one hand, and Minnie on the other.

At one point in the wee hours, Seb stirred. "Are you *crying?*" he whispered. "Don't worry, I'll go to urgent care tomorrow and get it scanned or whatever they do." Nels was embarrassed. Sebastian was quite aware of Nels' neuroticism, having known and loved him for many years. But even so. There was nothing worse than a cloying and maternal lover, was there? Nels didn't want to be anxious, but he kept seeing Minnie coughing and Seb choking, and the film in his mind kept turning through to the bitter end where they were both dead on the floor.

Sebastian had gone to the clinic that morning while Nels went to work. "You're not calling in sick," he said, knowing that Nels wanted to accompany him. "I'll be fine. I'm a big boy now."

While he waits for Seb's text which will come later, with scan results showing no blockage or aspiration, just a scratch in the pipe that will heal in a few days, Nels manages a handful of subsequent calls from Mrs. Morris, infamous at the office for her hypochondria. Today she has a twitch in her right eye, a persistent pain in her back that might be a pulled muscle from vacuuming but might be her kidneys, and another thing, some puffiness what looks like swelling under her chin and could be an inflamed thyroid.

Through the phone, Mrs. Morris could never see him rolling his eyes, but Nels has always penciled her in with a bit of impatience, assuming people like her are sad and needy attention seekers. Today he feels differently, and wonders, what if it was all true, the various pains, and something really was going wrong that no one could understand? Who hasn't experienced the unruly unravelling of the body, out of your control?

He realizes for the first time that her problem is fear, not the desire for attention. She is scared. What she wants is compassion from someone who knows how it all works and some professional assurance. And he thinks how we all want the same thing, after all, the affirmation that we are going to be okay, when we are not okay, because if we are okay, we are not going to be okay for long.

Snow Fall

after *Snow Storm,* by JMW Turner (England) 1842

In midnight snow, blue diamond moonshine. Your antlers hoisted skyward by January gales. Everything reckless and wilding. Your eyes, fearless deep glitter. As if you weren't something I was vanquishing.

Winter was for powdery almond crescents and Bailey's. Us sotted, bored. Shooting elastic bands and spit peas at Michael Snow's famous Eaton Centre geese mobile. We never thought you'd die. Ever. And not waving a white flag.

Look, an avalanche, the roiling tides under all those toboggans: the cold as hot and angry as a volcano. We were always wary of weather. Impudent, inclement. Sleet, sleigh bells. Everything coming down.

Vore

after The Broken Column, by Frida Kahlo (Mexico) 1944

The end is near. A whole life spanning war and peace, two continents, two farms, and two children has been reduced to a fetid bingo room with wheelchairs duelling for the front row. Mother slumps low. Her gnarled hands are pincers atop flabby pools of thigh. She squints to see at all, with only one blinking fish-eye still computing shape and shadow.

Lissa has grown more patient since learning that the thing consuming Mother is growing inside her, too. Already she is unsteady and her bones are softer. It is sometimes hard to find the words she needs, and she stumbles to recall simple details, taking longer to put sentences together. She relies on a cane and thick, sturdy shoes. Everything is swollen.

She puts a hand softly on her mother's elbow, about to remark on how they resemble each other, something she had never noticed until recently. Mother lashes her arm with amazing strength considering the dislocated shoulder. Hisses at Lissa to get her cotton-picking paws off of her. Lissa retreats into herself again, wonders why she bothers coming at all.

Mother's mouth opens and closes like a bass out of water. Where is Kyle? she rasps, leaking streaks of drool out the sides of her grimace. Mother is sweet on Kyle, who brings her coffee and pastels de nata when he visits. Lissa explains that he is at work tonight, and waits to hear a tirade about how lucky she is that she has a man who can stand her. But

Mother's mind is elsewhere this time. She sputters, finding steam, then out of nowhere, raises her voice for everyone to hear. "You better not be jumping into bed with that man and offending God," she warns.

It's been months, maybe longer, since Lissa and Kyle last made love. She was terrified of never connecting that way again. He was afraid of hurting her, even though the bruises were from falling, not from love. In her past life, she'd been wild and free, loved loving every which way, with all the lights on. It was different now, with crumbling joints and compression garments killing any hopes of romance. They slept side by side like old friends or siblings, with him helping her use the crutches to get to the toilet when things were really bad.

Lissa tries not to take it personally. Mother has always despised any notion of her children's romance. Not just love, but anything that might separate them from her. She hated their laughter. She hated their music. Their livelihood. Their lives. What she loved was their suffering. When Lissa first told her she was ill, too, Mother had not been able to hide that satisfied smile. Knowing she had passed on her pain for Lissa to endure was like winning the lottery. She could just sit back and watch her middle-age daughter disintegrating.

Lissa stands up slowly, easing onto her legs, careful not to wince or groan to give any indication of her pain. She steadies herself with her stick, wraps her spare arm carefully over Mother's bad shoulder. It is a strange sensation to touch her, a skeleton inside a flesh suit, all soft with sharp angles jutting through to the surface. For a moment, Mother holds her, too, squeezes her back. Lissa is just about to say she loves her, but holds back. Waits, hopes, that Mother will say it first.

Be careful on your feet, Mother says instead. Make sure you don't fall. It gets worse from here, a lot worse. Soon you'll be in this chair, too.

Leaving

after *Untitled,* by Zdzislaw Beksinski (Poland) 1978

Bank of the Old Mississippi. In the blinking lanterns and soft rain. They watch the dinner boats stream by. The jovial trombones and the big baritones ride the kaleidoscope currents. Night is eternal overhead, polished plush indigo, and just a crooked hook left of the moon.

Her head on his knees. The way she keeps saying to open his eyes and turn them skywards. He takes in the sweeping stars with her. Once, she showed him the impossibly blue-eyed sky over a tabasco and crawfish shack far away from the city.

He knows she'll go home. Not even the devil could make her stay. He could only invite her here and show her the ropes. And she likes those ropes. There's something dark and burned inside of her.

But even so, he understands, it's not the darkness that compels her. It's the light. She'll follow it when it moves her. He knows he is living on borrowed time. And so is she. She has some kind of blood sickness. Her time is finite. Too few of us are immortals. Soon she'll get her fill of too many Hurricanes and too much purple plastic. Her travels are all about seeing the world before it is consumed, while she still can.

One night he watched her filling a little empty baggie with cemetery dirt. Scooping the stuff straight up with her fingers. He found it elemental, her bare hands in the dirt like gardening only everything here dead. She wanted to keep it with her, everything that was gone.

There's a field fire, wild and primitive, visible from the distance and she wants to go. The pale ones are out there. They have broken mirrors in the trees, sending fragments of the blaze and the stars across the river. He warns her not to get bitten, but she laughs and says she's not afraid.

They slow dance in front of the fire. Broken blues on a broken radio. The palest of them all is stirring booze in a cauldron with a huge silver wand. They each pour a ladle full into their water vessels after taking a long swig. Someone's pounding a skin drum at the edge of the clearing.

It's way after the moon dissolves that the trolls stumble in. The energy changes. She thinks the vampires are beautiful, winged things, birds lost in time. Their evil doesn't frighten her. But these muddy creatures are rough trade from the mines to the east or far south, and she doesn't want the hassle. Their quarrels and brawls are not poetry, she says, because picking up lost teeth and slipping on viscera is not the same as fangs penetrating a throat or gifting eternity.

Come, she says, weaving her slender fingers around his, and they make their way back to the Quarter.

Her favourite perch in the corridors is an abandoned car sprouting ivy and daisies, in the shadows of the window of masks. She smokes and sips from her vessel and they watch the tourists going inside. She likes to guess which masks they might buy: ornately crafted Venetian leatherwork, or ceremonial wood carvings from Africa. The one she wanted most was a slender pistachio green Harlequin eye cover, plain and supple with slim slits for the mystery of her eyes. He fastened it for her, tenderly tucking her hair away from the knot.

"Look," she says. "I can't stay here forever." He's been waiting for this. She digs deeper. "You weren't expecting me to, I know that."

"What's it like there?" he asks, because there's nothing left to say and nothing that will change it. You can no more change the tides than you can change the fires.

"Mostly industrial now," she says. Describes the place: steel and skyscrapers and on the outskirts, acres after acres of charred trees, each one a pitchfork in the red skies.

"That doesn't sound like something to run to," he says, but she shrugs. "Home is home." If she has someone waiting for her, she doesn't say so.

He draws her closer. They savour the low and heavy humidity, the mournful wailing of the saxophone. "I'll miss this," she says, and tips her head back to swallow the flock of thin birds overhead with her eyes. She says it's very simple. She is homesick, nothing more or less.

There are a few surviving orchards there, she tells him after a long silence. And how that means hope. The cherry blossoms will be breaking into the bloom across the peninsula. And the strawberries in June: so round and sweet before summer.

The Place Behind the Orchard

after *Mourning Picture,* by Edwin Romanzo Elmer (USA)
1870

On an afternoon of clean cashmere clouds and heavy with
apples, a girl with a lamb came in from the orchards and
plunked herself beside me. She was spilling with stories
about meadows and rivers and a clapboard house. She had a
doll named Agatha, in a red and yellow buggy, and a pet
chicken, but she'd lost them along the way.

Along the way where? I asked her.

To *here,* she said. To here, from *there.*

I knew she wasn't there at all. I was an imaginative child
with many storybook friends who climbed out of the pages
of my favourite fairy tales and adventure novels. I called her
Effie and envied her titian tresses and pet sheep. She told me
about the place behind the orchard, a maze of long corridors,
where all kinds of people in funny costumes from the past
shuffled around with their heads down. Said she had snuck
away with Agatha and Patty and no one had even noticed.

I invited Effie inside to play Noah's Ark, using my bed as the
big boat for all of the plush animals. The floor was all terrible
gales and raging floods. Some days the two of us made tea
for the pets and toys instead, pouring creek water out of a
discarded Brown Betty with a broken spout. We played at
being fairies. We dressed Patty in old pajamas. We collected

lost marbles and made up our own rules for our games. We were happy together for so many summers that I lost count.

Effie didn't come to my tenth birthday party. She said the real girls would turn into mean girls if they saw her. And I never saw her again.

Some years later, my father was working seeds into soil that had once been the brook, and his shovel clinked against metal. He loosened the soil and pulled out some old carriage wheels with chips of red paint, and the remains of an old bisque doll.

Part of me leapt back in time, seized on those porcelain bones as proof…of something. The other part of me knew there were countless doll parts buried under the blankets of blossoms across New England. I was fifteen, old enough to know better, to fill my head with math and geography homework and daydreams for Jordache jeans and boys in Mustangs, instead of make-believe.

It was another lifetime later, me pushing a stroller with a cranky toddler inside, and dragging a husband through a museum for a little culture. We drove to an old gallery in a neighbouring town as a family excursion. I felt a desperate need for that intangible but essential thing you get from paintings or music, something other than dirty dishes and diapers and bills. I remembered visiting it with my folks when I was small.

I looked at small ivory carvings from the cold north, and tepid, floral flushes of soft oil. Nothing really spoke to me.

But then, there she was. A forgotten thing. An impossibility. Effie, in her rainbow piped corduroy smock, standing on the grass with that lamb. Patty. A drab and tidy house the colour of putty stood sturdy against the bluest sky, and a couple dressed in black robes rested soberly in the shade under it.

Her parents, in Victorian bereavement attire, while their little girl played on the front lawn.

Effie looked right past me down the glowing corridor. Then she caught my eye, and her expression changed, as if she recognized me, too.

I approached the placard, read the title. *Mourning Picture,* by Edwin Romanzo Elmer.

The museum notes explained. Elmer was a landscape painter with few known works. He painted this one in memory of Effie, his nine-year old daughter who died from a burst appendix, leaving her parents childless and heartbroken.

It was a painting of a ghost.

"Mama," my son burbles, until I finally surface from my astonishment and return to the present. A strange prickle moves over my skin when I retrieve his black and white toy cat from the gallery floor. "Cow," he says, what he named his stuffed animal, pointing towards Effie. He grins at her. In the painting, her little cat is the same as the one he is holding.

Mark has moved on to a wall of ripening fruit with wasps and chalices and broken violins. My son, clutching Cow, turns in his stroller to catch a last glimpse of Effie and her cat. He opens and closes his little fingers, waving goodbye as if they are old friends.

Films About Ghosts

after *Horse and Train,* by Alex Colville (Canada) 1954

After the stroke, your Oma's personal effects, the only photograph of your uncle. Baby-faced and black-haired, like Elvis. You stare at those deep dark wells, run your fingers over his cable knit sweater. You have no memories of John except the photograph. Still, you see the familiar film in your mind's eye, the train bearing down the tracks, the desperate jumping. How Mother wielded him dangly and bloody over grandmother to get her way. All three of them dead, now, all three still like strangers. Mother's brother a pawn of her ugly fury, of her insatiable loneliness.

Flicker

after *Coyotes Came Out of the Desert*, by Matsusaburo
George Hibi (USA, b. Japan) 1945

The towers pile light-buzzing screens one on top of the other,
like static interference, like flickering binary code. Kate isn't
quite sure what she was expecting from a quantum frequency
healing circle, but it wasn't a bunch of heavily made-up
women in capris and cheap little white slippers.

She sighs and leans back in the cheap lawn chair, but it's not
easy to relax under the assault of fluorescent light tracks
overhead. Each glowing tube is amplified by the endless cold
glare of the walls. She had assumed that the scalar wave
treatment clinic would be more ambient, perhaps, like a yoga
studio, with a warm tangle of spider plants and a laughing
Buddha statue. The only art on the wall is an illustration of
the spiritual body with squiggly rays, but it doesn't look
cosmic at all, more like a police chalk outline of a murder
victim.

The lone man in the room strikes does look like the serial
killers she's seen interviewed on TV, gaunt and awkward
with Coke bottle glasses and sunken eyes. When she looks
in his direction, he is already staring at her, lower lip lax and
slippery. She represses a shiver. He must be ill, she thinks.
Not a stretch, of course- all of them are sick and desperate,
hoping for a miracle potion, or a magic wand, a flicker of
transformative biofield energy. For him, it must be cancer.

It's the way his skin barely covers his ribs or even cheekbones, and the strange sporadic ruddy darkness of him.

Kate looks away, and her eyes fall on the woman who is sharing. Electric curly hair. The glow of her face reveals she is a true believer. "We are MADE of light," the woman says emphatically. "Our bodies know how to heal themselves! But we suppress our own innate wisdom! These flickering photons can reset our frequencies."

Nods and murmurs flutter up from the circle. For a few moments Kate drifts in the silence. She wonders briefly if she is finally feeling the energy. There is a fleeting sense of alignment and a pleasant pressure at the base of her spine. The brochure promised she didn't need faith: the flickering screens would work whether you believed it or not. Was this the start of the shift from chronic pain to wholeness?

In another moment she knows the warm tingling is a more commonplace matter. She has to pee. Rats! How long can she hold out? There are no phones in the healing space, and nothing so earthly and banal as a clock on the wall. Time is, of course, just a construct. But how can she assess what's left of the hour, and whether her bladder can hold that long?

Someone else shares a testimony of transformation. This woman had been told she needed a blood transfusion after a long weakness resulting from toxic chemotherapy. She started taking iron and B12 to rebuild her blood. She took the Neulasta injection they recommended, too, to help her restore her platelets. And she came to just one hour of energy enhancement before this! When she went to her appointment, they told her she no longer needed the transfusion.

After the first flicker session, the woman explains, she had visualized her blood cells knitting back together. And then she could feel it happening. Deep inside, she knew she no would no longer need the procedure.

Kate wonders which course of action was really to thank for her recovery. She wonders how the rays the screens are transmitting can be energizing when the desktop and smartphone waves are toxic. The overhead fluorescents are triggering her migraines now. She feels a thin piercing drill starting deep inside her skull and knows it will build into a killer event if she doesn't relax and find soft natural light soon.

A woman with big brassy hair and tattooed eyebrows is sharing now. She is as round as a ball and has a shiny nose. She discovered the realm of rainforest shamanism years ago, in university, reading anthropology from Carlos Castaneda. His work opened her eyes to the profound possibilities that ancient cultures understood.

Kate recalls her own infatuation with the psychedelic guru during college. She'd devoured everything he said, hook, line and sinker. When it came out later that he'd made it all up, she was gutted, and embarrassed to have been so gullible. Even after the indigenous leaders, genuine shamans of Mexico, corrected the record and accused him of fabrication and appropriation, some people still represented his experiences as truth instead of a hoax. What was objective reality, after all, but one facet of mystery among many?

Kate leans back into the lawn chair, tries again to sense waves of love and enlightenment, to feel the positive healing frequencies in her spine instead of just the increasingly necessary signals to urinate. She still wants to believe that the only obstacle between her turning at will into a crow or soaring swallow is the church and state repressing her true nature. Morphine and cortisone and Gabapentin have all failed her, so what is left, if not the hope there are other ways to overcome the constant burning in her nerves? As the migraine starts to flood over her, she closes her eyes again. She imagines herself outside of the pain, floating in the white flashing fields, talking to wild coyotes.

Frost

after *View of Rooftops (Effects of Snow),* by Gustave Caillebotte (France) 1879

The cold gray span of morning, the season's second snow. We watch the weary world from our warm window, as winter settles softly on the city's sloping roofs. Jane taps her vague reflection in the frosty glass, ghostly against the shuttered dormers across the way. She blinks hard, turns. She is crying again and I move aside to give her the space she needs.

Her hair was gone fast, barely a week after the first round of poison. We assumed it would be gradual. More recently, her eyebrows and eyelashes thinned close to bare. She hid both behind trendy oversized glasses.

I'll make the coffee, I tell her. In a few minutes, I pour my promise from the percolator into her favourite mug, take it to her. Jane is standing in front of the mirror. I'm used to her this way already- if anything, she is even more beautiful to me. But she describes her loss as something violent and violating, like watching the years flowing down the drain. Says her independence and strength and desire have been ripped from her skull against her will.

I think she is thinking about this now, but she turns and tells me a different story. I just had a strange memory, she says, while looking at myself. When I was in college I had an unusual roommate. He was very beautiful but strange. His skin was milky and veiny, kind of translucent. Ethereal. He was a diva, sort of. Flamboyant but very timid. He wore the finest, pointiest kidskin shoes. He wore fake Hermes scarfs, with an array of knots, around his neck. He had nothing in the fridge except plain yogurt and Evian water. I wondered if he had an eating disorder. The weirdest thing, his wigs, glossy and silver or blue, meticulous, constructed haircuts. Hanging on the walls of his room… they were like icicles, and like tarantulas crawling there!

A lot of us in college had unusual obsessions, so I just let him be.

Jane pauses, takes her coffee back to the window to watch the snow starting again, to look over the city she is so disconnected from now. The glass is glittery with shards of ice. She taps the window again, waves for my attention. Then she goes on. See, I saw myself this morning here, and across the years, out of the reflection, I saw him looking back at me. He was always so perfectly penciled, carefully coiffed. But in the mornings, I was surprised by how bare he was without makeup. His eyes were practically naked. His real hair was as thin and pale as a baby's. I never connected the dots. It's just the way he was. We got on just fine but lost touch after school. Truth be told, I forgot all about him.

Until this morning. Jane saw him staring back at her, across time. As if it was me, she says. But how could I know the signs way back when? She shivers. Presses a fingertip against the glass. Why was it a secret? she wonders. Something to carry alone? He must have been so cold.

No Fixed Address

after *Gray and Gold,* by John Rogers Cox (USA) 1942

Same old jeans, and oh, still so fine inside them. Much softer, all those jagged edges sanded by these years between us. And still tough as nails. Of course. Eyes part mean, part mystery. Those hands, everywhere they've been. On bar rails and dancing poles, on the gear shift, on apples and branches and the freshly upturned earth. All over all those pyramids across Mexico. Brilliant and brutal on your guitar. If you wanted me to know where you went and where you've been, you would have told me, so I didn't ask. I know you married. Some guy from the city with the country in his boots, the perfect fit for everything you are and everything will be. Well, it was me who ran and left you open to the future, but I was just returning to you what you were going to take from me. I didn't want to tie you down and hold you back with all the things that were wrong with me. I knew we weren't going to be the only ones in our stories. More than anything, I wanted to give you back to the road.

Disgust

after *Old Woman Bleeding a Young Woman*, by Quiringh van Brekelenkam (Netherlands) 1660

Mother is helpless now, her old body twisted and trapped. A place she's never been. Age has almost tamed her. She is the ghost of her former ruthlessness. She is almost not there at all.

I'm shocked by the decline since my last visit a few weeks ago. Mottled, bruised, flesh coming loose from the bones. When she hears my voice, she turns to find me with her best eye, the other one wobbling in the opposite direction. "You finally came," she rasped. "Glad you could take some time out of your busy schedule."

Her breath is sour and her lips are scabbed. Her flabby breasts flop to either side of her and the whole room smells like piss. I feel a wave of revulsion. As if she can read my mind, she says, "Not afraid of a bit of pee, are you, dear? Because I'm going right now." And she gives that familiar signature snigger, still mocking us, even from her diapers.

After awhile, she asks, "Where are my Cheetos?"

She wants to devour whatever is cheap, salty, and she wants it now.

Earlier she had called my brother, demanding he swing by the home with a bag of cheese puffs. He said he was at work and would bring them with him later. "You stupid fool," she had hissed at him. "You never could lift a finger for your

Mother." He had called me then and told me I was on my own for the visit.

She doesn't even ask about my brother.

Mother keeps patting the bed with her spindly hand, wanting me to sit next to her. Getting too close to her has felt repugnant for as far back as I can remember, even as I have longed for a scrap of intimacy or approval. I say I'm fine in the chair, giving her more room to be comfortable.

There wasn't much else to talk about. There never had been.

I think about the waste of her life. Now she's approaching the finish line with nothing to show for it. Not one person besides us has come to visit her here. She routinely burned through any friends she'd had. And the destruction of my father was long complete. She danced on his grave.

I scan the past, desperate to land on a pleasant memory, something with affection or wonder or laughter. But any fleeting snapshot of joy is quickly punctuated with whatever followed it. Cruelty, chaos, manipulation.

The idea that a whole life can go by without even a slight shift of insight or softening or regret feels like an open wound.

"You're not crying, are you?" Mother says, not bothering to hide her disgust. She pushes a handful of already-soggy tissues my way. "Dry those crocodile tears, for crying out loud, Missy." Words I haven't heard for many decades.

I fiddle with the dial on her radio, find some buoyant jazz to change the mood. "Turn that noise off," Mother says. We sit in silence. After another while, she asks for her hairbrush. I feel that one beady eye working to follow my footsteps. I rummage on the cluttered dresser top. Cringe when my hand lands on her dentures.

I hand the brush to her, but she shakes her head. "You do it," she says. Her hair is thin and soft and slimy and I see her ruddy, scaly scalp through the translucent strands. I swallow my repulsion and begin stroking her skull gently with the brush. Her glassy eyes start to water. She is crying, too. "Is it hurting your head, Mama?" I ask gently. She shakes her head again. "It's just been so long since anyone has touched me," she says.

Pica

after Cannibals, by Odd Nerdrum (Norway) 2005

The man with wheels growing from his thighs takes his raw in his bare hands. Straight up, still bleeding. His daughter uses both hands. The fiends come up from the fires when the hunger strikes. They look for the fattest ones among us.

We avoided them for a long while. We avoided all of it. Retreated into the maze of cubicles. The water coolers were still gurgling long after the parched river beds had gasped their last. The blinking screens held us in thrall so we couldn't tell what was real. If we didn't leave, we couldn't see the sky. We couldn't see anything.

Our scouts confirmed the truth about the fiends. Their camps under the bridge, our carcasses left heaped across the refuse mounds like graffiti.

When the vending machines and all the freezers were finally emptied, we moved to desperate measures. There was a flat of non-alcoholic beer and a bulk barrel of blue gummy whales. It would buy us a week at most, and then what?

The long one, tied in knots and fluttering bandanas, paces from one abandoned desk to another, wrenching every drawer open. He finds an ancient batch of red Twizzlers, lean and delicate like dehydrated jerky. A cut-glass crystal bottle, still half full of bourbon.

Finders, keepers. He tips the neck to his narrow lips, drains a few fingers. Feeling generous, he passes it along.

The next in line runs his tongue over the slatted glass. "Do you ever crave mirror shards?" he asks. "Broken glass mulch. Metal shavings. It's some disease you get when you go nutty. People eat screws and gravel."

We all eye the supply mountain in the middle. Not much on it but blank post it notes and staples. Stubby small pencils that once starred in games of office bingo. Our glances flicker lustfully back to the bottle of booze.

"My cat had that," one pipes in. "A riddle of a thing. The wee beast would go to town on the plaster. She would suck on wires and when I left a wrench in the driveway after fixing a wheel, found her chewing on it."

He shrugs. Gets wistful. "Well, shit, the thing was twice her size."

And he starts weeping.

"Did'ya eat 'er?" shouts the office joker. Erupts into maniacal laughter.

"I think pica is when you're starving for meat," someone offers. "It's a mistake, what they did once to people with nails in their intestines. They didn't know. If you can't convert the proteins, you start looking in your coin purse for zinc and iron."

"Well, now then," says another. "On the old farm. The cows got this thing. They loved to eat frozen fences. Bessie would graze on green grass and railway ties given the chance."

"There aren't no cows left in the whole world," says someone else.

I never say a word. I just watch. The time for opinions is long over.

Every week or so, the ones with a scrap of strength remaining will pull the fallen to the service elevator. We might bang on trash cannisters or fold neon yellow post-its into origami. For some kind of ritual or service, to mark their ending somehow. They leave them for the fiends to clean their bones and hope they'll be appeased when out making their rounds. The fiends prefer their meat fresh, though, and if they take too long in scrounging the environs, the fallen become fodder for coyotes and creeping things. Whatever vultures remain.

I'd been hiding some tubes of paint among a sack of rotten potatoes stowed from the fry factory in the cafeteria. Sucking on them when everyone else was distracted. Umber, ochre, parchment. I was careful to rinse myself clean of birch and bronze streaks after. Not willing to share. Eventually, they would come for the stash: rancid, rotten, so? One more day and the odds were getting shorter. There were boils in my liver, anyways, festering cysts and scars that would soon be dust.

My mind returns to the room. Someone is confessing they ate meat, torn off the third-floor secretary a day after she fell. There was still salt and soy sauce from packets under the stairs. She'd done what she had to. And now?

There are only moments more. Days, maybe, for a few lucky ones. The end is nigh no matter how you roll the dice.

The stale booze is medicine. It's just the dregs when it reaches me, but I take it. Every last drop.

Then I crack the bottle in my bare fist. Use my other hand as the shovel, spoon a crunch of crystals shards. Raise them to my open mouth.

Shamrock

after *Mt. Vernon Woman,* by Palmer C. Hayden (USA) 1950

No one would turn their heads back or whistle at the woman on the subway platform, no one, that is, but Collins. Her demeanor was somewhat plain. She was dressed nicely enough, in an understated way, blending in with hundreds of other nice, average women on their way home from work. Slightly chubby, brunette. He could tell by the blooming apron of her lower belly that she was on the middle to high end of forty even though her face read late 30s. The extra flesh was slowly starting to ease its way loose from the bone. This would rule her out for some and count her in for others, depending what it was a man was looking for.

Collins didn't care if they were fat or skinny. He liked a tumble of curls, or a thick straight sheath of shiny. Black or blonde, no matter, even salt and pepper pleased him equally. He liked them in jeans, pant suits, or skirts. So long as they wore sandals. That's what it was he saw first when he looked at her. Her feet were strong and wide and sturdy, confident in practical Clarks. Her ankles were chunky enough to hold her thickening frame. But her toenails were perfectly coiffed in a dreamy pale peach polish and her arch was the rival of any ballerina's. He was smitten instantly.

He imagined unveiling her. Taking his time with the buckle. Feeling the puffy ankle with his fingers, trailing them over the slim spaces between the sweet and tubby toes.

If he was occasionally ashamed of his gawking, he forgave himself. He was hardly the worst among men. And since Jill had gotten sick with esophageal cancer, leaving him too soon, he'd been so isolated.

The woman turns, says something he can't catch. He looks up, finds a face as warm and intelligent as her more pedestrian pleasures.

"What's that, sorry?" Collins motions to the din around them and to his ear, tries on a friendly smile of his own. "Oh, I was just asking, are you a poet?" the woman with the beautiful toes replies. She points at the library book he is carrying. Modern Irish poets.

He catches her eye now. Feeling more comfortable. She has tiny lines around her eyes and mouth, and something about the shared humanity of it feels intimate to him. He crinkles his nose, grins. "Sort of," he says. "Sometimes." She asks to take a peek.

Maybe she's married or a mother or busy or otherwise taken. But Collins takes a chance. Asks if she'd like to get a drink with him. He knows there is a cozy pub not far from the next stop, the Shamrock. She smiles again, toothy and kind and cute for days. She shrugs a shy acceptance with one shoulder. Taps a finger against a page, Kavanagh, where he has underlined some lines twice.

"I love this poem," she says.

The Asylum for Idiots and Imbeciles*

after *The New Asylum for Idiots,* by Edmund Evans (England) 1854

**Historical note: This offensive and ableist name was a standard variation of like names in the 1800s for institutions throughout the USA, Canada, and the UK.*

After the divorce, Jesse dusted off her ancient Nikon and started taking pictures. Her phone was better and faster, but she liked being forced to make choices about what she snapped, having a finite number of options. The sense of rarity about it changed the way she framed things. She also liked the surprise of what came back to her from the lab. Jesse was pretty sure the next step was developing them herself. The darkroom, that patience and solitude, held a certain romance for her.

But things took an unexpected turn. Instead of retreating into the artist's lonely space, something she'd longed for over for decades, she found herself on a noisy and crowded mini-bus with the urban explorers' club, headed north out of the city.

Jesse's seatmate wants to talk shop, asks about what abandoned factory or asylum she found most moving as a photographer. She gives up on being alone among many, and drifts into comfortable conversation with Ed. She admits she is new to this. The Asylum for Idiots and Imbeciles is her first run.

Jesse just happened to see the flyer posted at the library when she was returning some mystery novels. It was a camera club, with photographers who had a special interest in local ruins. They were going to a long ago home for an aunt of an aunt she'd never known who'd been taken there because she was feeble of mind and of body, too. Though she'd never felt a particular kinship with or longing for Aunt Jane, the hideous name of the hospital had always stuck in her craw.

When Jesse's breasts were amputated, thick keloid scars raised like ropy kudzu vines across her flat chest as quickly as she had once grown those delicate teacup buds. With Jim gone God knows where, barely able to look at her, she'd thought of her old aunt, who had festered to death with her female troubles in a godforsaken home run by nuns. When she finally pulled her camera out, she named it Jane without really knowing why chose to do so.

This is the story she tells Ed, since he is listening. And being heard is not something she's used to. She is sorry for wanting to shut him out when she first nabbed one of only a few free seats. Everyone looked like they already knew each other, and Ed looked a bit like a redneck, and she had judged his overbite and the gangly fit of his pants. Now she thinks he looks like a scarecrow, and she wants to photograph him in dry fields with a copper cannon sun sinking behind him.

She doesn't know, can't know, what he is thinking, thinking about her, too. How he wants to turn his own camera on her scars. Make a record of her soul and body finally freed, the fork in the road before her.

It's a tragedy, Ed says, where we're going. What they named them, and what they did to people who were different or disabled. He also tells her about his time on Manitoulin Island, snapping long grass growing through some vacant old stone church window arches.

Jesse doesn't know that within a few months, she will trade in her casual capris and flowy cowl neck blousons for vintage Lee jeans and ankle biter hiking boots. She will sport Tilley vests with an array of pockets for her gear. She will climb over stone walls and under bramble vines and carefully snap the way the slatted light moves over the barred windows of an old labour prison. She doesn't know how tough she will get, or how adrenaline will carry her, over padlocked walls where barking dogs brandish rows of gleaming daggers. How she will find that solitary flower or that lost tiny toy bird. How she, with her hopelessly old-fashioned film, will capture those small promises, those brave but long forgotten disappointments of hope.

Nerve

after *The Surgeon,* by David Teniers the Younger (Belgium)
1670

The pain ripping through her teeth was a forest fire, a dagger
digging under every molar, incisor, and fang. Noor was tired
of bringing it up. The futility hurt more. It was always the
same. "Have you seen a dentist?" "Yes." And then, her, at
first delicately, and then with increasing frustration,
attempting to educate the medical classes. The pain began
after surgery on her ankle. It was acute and monstrous, like
a scream. Three, two, one… "But we operated on your leg,
not your jaw." "Thanks for clarifying, Doc, I'd forgotten."
"Don't get smart. I'm trying to help you." When Noor had a
cortisone shot for arthritis, she'd felt the long, terrible needle
work itself into her ankle joint- on the opposite foot. She felt
the pain from the surgery there, but also in her hips, hands,
and teeth. "If you want to help, please listen to me and what
I'm telling you instead of checking off items in your chart,"
she pleaded. From his response, he clearly didn't hear her.
"Noor, I'm reluctant to give you hydromorphone again," he
rattled predictably. If he'd bothered reading that damn chart,
he'd see she wasn't interested and had had no relief from
previous attempts. "Don't you have something else in your
arsenal?" she pleaded. "Nerve blockers or something like
that?" But the doctor started yapping about a group that
meets on Wednesdays to do breathing and visualization
exercises. "Would that be your choice?" she asked. He
looked startled, then his eyes glazed over again. "Excuse

me?" "Would that be your choice, if you were me, in excruciating acute pain after a major ankle surgery? Waiting until Wednesday, finding a ride in, and picturing pretty flowers blowing in the breeze?" The intensity in her gums was so wicked that she could taste gravel and stainless steel. Noor's left hand also began throbbing. Strange, it was the same whenever she heard piercing sirens or heavy bass reverb, the fingers she'd broken when she was fifteen began to hammer. She'd slammed it in the car door on her way to track over forty years ago. At the time, she didn't feel a thing.

Minnows

after *Lake Keitele*, by Akseli Gallen-Kallela (Finland)1905

First things first: Alice plugs in the percolator, pulls a couple of mugs out of the cupboard, takes out the honey and the cream. She savours the heady earthy scent especially this morning, after polishing off nearly a bottle of Riesling herself the night before. Emma had arrived with an impressive array of vintages from the city.

Emma is still sleeping, of course, not accustomed to the invitation of the dawn warblers or the lake country air. Alice tastes the coffee, then carries it down to the water, where she wades among water lilies, watching the minnows. She has not tired of this morning ritual, immersing her ankles in the warmer months, in the years since she bought a cow and some hens and an old fixer-upper.

She was glad to see Emma, even though her old friend only bothers to visit when she's in the throes of another heartbreak. Emma prefers Alice's quarterly visits to the city, since pulling out the futon is much easier than making the drive herself. Emma is the kind of friend who gushes her affection and breathlessly declares that she would do anything for you, but never does.

When Alice was losing Gary, the long agony of his early decline was something she soldiered through alone. For two terrible years he coughed and coughed, while Alice tried to soothe the spasms and make him more comfortable. Watching him struggle for breath was the most painful thing

Alice had ever experienced, and she would sometimes close the bathroom door, turn on the water, sit herself on the edge of the tub, and weep into a towel.

On one of those occasions, she had texted her old friend and asked her to come and stay over. She was unimaginably lonely at that moment and needed a friend. She'd envisioned Emma sweeping in late and changing swiftly into flowy pajamas while Alice poured some wine. They would sit on the balcony and look over the city without saying much of anything.

But Emma had texted back that she wouldn't be able to sleep properly with Gary's laboured breathing. Why didn't Alice join her tomorrow at the hot new little bistro downtown, when the PSW came by, and give herself a break from all of it?

If Alice felt that her friend was thoughtless and self-absorbed, Gary was more generous. "Some people just can't be there for you in the ways you would like," he said once, "because they can't face themselves, even if it seems like that's all they think about."

That's what Alice remembers as she wiggles her toes in the slick sand, shooing the nibbling sunfish into a tangle of sea vines. Last night they had chilled the wine right here among the shimmering minnows and the rocks. They had listened to the water for a long time in comfortable silence, watching the moon rise and the stars whoosh across the plush blue night.

After a bottle had gone dry, Emma had sobbed until she was empty. This time, she'd learned that an old flame she'd once been crazy about had remarried. He'd been married at the time of the affair between them, but he wouldn't leave his wife for her. Now, she had learned through some colleagues, he had left his wife. Not for her but for someone else.

Alice had thought at the time that a man who carried on with another woman while he was with the one he claimed to love would do exactly the same thing in another circumstance. A man like that was no prize. It was the best outcome for everyone, she'd thought. Emma had moved on, too, finding other ways to get her heart broken.

This particular affair had been way before Gary died, but the news felt to Emma like a fresh betrayal. As she sniffled that every man she'd ever dated was a dog, just out to use her, Alice wondered if the problem with everybody Emma knew was Emma.

She understood then how at least part of the reason she had moved to the wilderness was to be farther away from her friend. This was true even though she missed her friend, and all the drama, and everything they did together, all the exhibitions and film festivals and dinners in the city.

Emma is coming with her java, stumbling down the pathway awkwardly in her ivory peignoir and marabou slippers, like a forgotten movie star. Her eyes are still puffy, but she smiles and touches Alice's arm when she reaches the water.

"Thanks so much for last night," she says in that familiar husky voice. "It was good to talk it out."

They both sip their coffees. After awhile, Emma slithers out of her mules and joins Alice in the shallow waters. Alice starts to laugh. The reflection in the lake, Emma in her French robe, dangling starlet ostrich slippers from one hand, is ridiculous and lovely.

"Well, I should get dressed," Alice says after awhile. "I'll feed the chickens and then I'll make breakfast. We can have pancakes, or just toast and smoked salmon?"

They stand a bit longer watching the minnows in the weeds. "They look so easy to catch," Emma says, and puts her hand into the water, and they're all gone elsewhere suddenly. She laughs.

Perhaps it is how everything is, Alice thinks briefly. How love, how time, how life, are like minnows, how everything slips and slides away so swiftly through your fingers.

All That She Wants

after *Trying on Necklaces,* by Delphin Enjolras (France)
before 1945

Dad was whisking a stir fry at the stove, but the soy sauce
and mustard medley of meat and green beans could not
compete with the cloud of strawberry bubbles overflowing
from the bathtub. Mother never closed doors and I'd caught
a glimpse of her oiling up a calf and pointed foot. She was
like a mermaid there in the heaps of white soap clouds.
Candles flickered against the mirrored walls like church and
Mom was singing along with some old-fashioned music.

We had just started dinner when Mother sidled into the
kitchen, perfumed, hair-sprayed, lipstick and little mirror in
one hand and high heeled strappy sandals in the other. Of
course we had set a place for her, maybe habit, maybe hope,
but she just tilted her neck the way in that way she had and
smiled. "Oh, no, thank you darlings," she said to me and my
sister. "I don't want to spoil my appetite. James knows the
most amazing little Spanish seafood spot." She daubed her
mouth with her favourite red lipstick. "Really, Alan?" she
said when she was finished. "You couldn't pour me a glass
of Chablis to sip while I'm waiting for my ride?"

Dad got flustered and opened and closed the fridge, stumbled
with his bad leg over the Dora knapsack I left on the floor.
He rubbed his hip briefly. He finally found a corkscrew and
opened a new bottle for Mother. I saw something like agony

on his face but he smiled, handed her a generous glass, and started chopping up a cucumber for our salad.

"How do I look, girls?" Mom asked, patting her hair. She was glamorous like a movie star in her sparkly, low-cut dress. The doorbell rang before I could tell her so. We saw James' fancy red car in the driveway and his feet, from the bottom window on the door. His shoes were black and glossy and I couldn't see anything else even though I ran to the door, nothing except James patting my mother's butt as casually as if she was his wife and not Dad's.

Jenny dug into her string beans with gusto. She stuffed her mouth full and then let some of the beans dangle between the holes in her front teeth, shrieking with laughter. Dad poured us some chocolate milk, my favourite, but we only get it when Mom has date night. Dad made amazing flavours from around the world out of his cookbook collection every night, but we usually got water or plain milk. He didn't like us having too much sugar.

Once I asked Mom why she didn't do the cooking and stuff around the house, to help Dad, since he was the one who went to work, not her. I thought that he could use the help, after the car accident that crushed his left side. It made sense to me that Dad should do less, and not more, and that Mom would want to help out because he was always in pain.

I couldn't describe the cold anger that came into her eyes then. "Your father can't take care of me now." She said it like she was spitting out something disgusting. "I mean, look at him. He's lucky I'm still here at all. The least he can do is look after his own children."

Later when I was reading Curious George to Jenny, I heard Dad talking on the phone with Oma while he put stuff into the dishwasher. I wasn't sure why he told her that Mother is at night school, because Mom didn't go to school. They were still talking when Jenny nodded off, so I went into the bathroom to get ready for bed.

Mom left her makeup out on the counter along with a few pairs of dangly earrings. I put the pink gloss on my lips and made a kissy face. I pulled my hair back and held the earrings to my lobes, and wondered if I'll ever look as beautiful as she does.

When I turned around, Dad was standing in the doorway. His leg must have been acting up because he looked like he was about to cry. He came over and took the earrings and put them back on the counter. He said Oma will have us over on Saturday and I hoped we would get to watch *Love Boat* with her and eat Froot Loops in front of the TV. Then Daddy fished my Jellycat rabbit from the living room. He brought her to my bed and tucked us in.

Appetite For Deconstruction

for Yves Klein 1928-1962

1. The world was not enough. At nineteen, he claimed the sky. At the beach with friends. Poked his forefinger up into the beyond, and signed his name. Mine, he said.

2. Yves Klein wanted to mainline the sky, the one that shimmered between day and nighttime, into his veins. He bled blue. He was not satisfied with the natural pigments available for painting. Like an alchemist of old, he fiddled and tinkered, abandoning nature for artifice and new technologies. A mad scientist. He invented the blue that blazed on the back of his eyelids when he shut them tight. He created hundreds of work using only International Klein Blue. He took his recipe to the grave, but science detectives have deciphered it: pigment, pure ultramarine blue, reference 1311, with pharmaceutic resin Rhodopas M60A from Rhone-Poulenc.

3. Klein's approach and his vision were as unlimited as the infinite that he'd claimed with his signature. He was not interested in creating anything that had already been created.

4. Could a painter paint without touching the canvas? Indeed. Art could be as performative as opera or porn. Klein created his Anthropometries as conductor. He staged the affair with beautiful naked models as his living brushes. He dipped them into vats of his blue. He waved his magic wand and they writhed on paper and canvas. "I stayed clean. I no

longer dirtied myself with colour, not even the tips of my fingers."

5. *Seiryoku zen'yō*: 精力善用: a concept in Judo. *Maximum efficiency, minimum effort.*

6. Blue martinis were served to help soak up the shock of the guests.

7. Composer, too. More than a decade before Warhol made his six-hour film reels of people sleeping, Klein created his Monotone Symphonies, consisting of twenty minutes of a single note, followed by twenty minutes of silence. Swiss trombonist Roland Dahinden recalled that they could not rehearse their music. "It's too hard. Everyone would just die."

8. In 2021, Italian artist Salvatore Garau raised a few eyebrows when he sold an invisible sculpture for $18000. But there is nothing new under the sun: the idea had been done to death already. Warhol had a nearly identical statue, with nothing on top of a pedestal: Invisible Sculpture, 1985. Klein was decades ahead of him. His exhibition of deconstruction, *Zone of Immaterial Pictorial Sensibility, or The Void,* was inspired by studies of Zen Buddhism. Klein sold documentation of ownership for blank spaces, then asked the buyer to participate in ritual burning of the papers.

9. Three thousand people waited in line to be let inside an empty room. The art show about nothing.

10. Today anyone can buy nothing. And for thirty bucks, you can buy a star and name it. A little piece of Yves Klein's sky.

11. Before all this, there was more. The artist was a yodan, or judo master, honoured at the Kodokan in Japan at the age of 25, the first European to achieve this rank. Klein wrote the book on it: *Les Fondements de Judo.*

12. Dojo life went hand in hand with amphetamines. A tragic interpretation of *Seiryoku zen'yō,* perhaps, but popular at the time.

13. In 1962, Klein married one of his living brushes, German model, muse, and artist Rotraut Uecker. They were expecting their first son when he had his first heart attack, experienced while watching a film by Gualtiero Jacopetti that featured some of his work.

14. He was thirty-four years old. Another heart attack followed soon after, and then another. *Un, deu, trois:* three strikes, you're out.

Epiphany

after *Portrait of a Young Woman*, by Maria Blanchard
(Spain) 1925

You're beautiful, I say to the young girl working the
supermarket checkout line. A habit I acquired after the hair
that I had worked for years to grow shiny and long came out
in one terrible weekend like clumps of seaweed in the
shower. After the plain face I had always taken for granted
blew up like a bowling ball from the prednisone. I mourned
that demise even as I gave thanks to have survived what so
few do. The habit of telling others wouldn't leave me. It felt
like something I should have always done. You're beautiful,
I say to the young girl working the supermarket checkout
line, because her dark face is wide and strong and her smile
is shy, and because maybe she is too young to know it yet,
and because maybe no one has ever told her.

Arsenic

after *Jason and Medea,* by John William Waterhouse
(England) 1907

1. "I don't want to die," former Alabama waitress Rhonda
Belle Martin said in the days before she was led to the
electric chair at the Kilby Correctional Facility. The year was
1957. "I want a chance to live." It's what we all want: that
pink crest of dawn clawing its way back from oblivion. The
promise and possibility of a new day.

2. It's what her victims wanted, too. Another chance, another
sunrise. How many did she snuff out with her arsenic and old
lace? Even Rhonda couldn't remember.

3. Did she think of the children as she dipped her cinnamon
roll into her coffee, at her last supper? Did she see the face
of her mother in the grinds or the crumbs, Mother, whose
coffee she had poisoned?

4. Rhonda admitted to killing several of her seven children.
She also killed her second husband. She married her fifth and
last husband after killing her fourth, his father.

5. She tried to kill him, too. Slowly, the way she liked it. He
refused to die. The ant poison crippled him. Paraplegic in a
chair. She liked that, too. The neediness and dependency. She
enjoyed tending the sick.

6. Her husband/step-son in the hospital is how she finally got
caught. There were too many questions.

7. She got a taste for the poison as a young mother. "The first time, I used insect poison my stepdaddy had under the house. I just got the urge and I suddenly did it." Her daughter was four years old and did not survive.

8. All seven of her children died, suddenly, or after various mysterious illnesses. Rhonda confessed to a handful of them. The others were investigated but not proven. She said her first daughter was born disabled. The *Montgomery Advisor* quoted her. "I never let that little girl get out of my sight. I cared for Adelaide day and night for three years until she died a natural death. Soon after she died, another of my children died a natural death." The paper questioned whether her mind snapped after the trauma. The truth was probably something different, and too terrible to bear.

9. *Factitious disorder imposed on another; Munchausen by proxy.* Rhonda was arrested in 1956. The syndrome wasn't named or discussed until 1977. A sadistic form of child abuse where a parent, usually the mother, feigns the illness of a child. She may convince the child they are ill and cannot play or socialize normally. She may inflict illness on them by injuring them or poisoning them. Milder versions mean a moderately sick child. It is quite common for her to kill her child, then have more kids so she can do it again and again.

10. She gets off on her victim's complete dependence and submission, on being needed, on visits to the doctor, on the thin line between life and death, and most of all, on the sympathy from others like doctors or neighbours. They see

her as a good, caring mother, unjustly afflicted with pain and responsibility. She loves the attention.

11. Assumed to be rare, one in a million. Newer studies suspect it's more like one in two hundred. No one dares suspect the truth when they see it, entangled in everything we think of as good and pure and nurturing. Hidden in plain sight. No one suspects a loving wife and mother, or a grieving one.

12. Experts and the prosecution were looking for motivations they could understand. They said she killed for the insurance money. The payout for one husband was around $500.

13. She said she found prison to be full of nice and caring people, not like the stereotypes. The staff was wonderful. She was herself very nurturing to the other inmates who looked up to her as the mother they never had. Just as she had enjoyed looking after sick neighbours and her disabled daughters, she enjoyed the opportunity to make a difference inside those walls. She also received a lot of letters and cards from people who read about the murders. "I have more friends now than I've ever had."

14. Rhonda took care of everything in advance of her date of execution. She would be buried in the Montgomery cemetery, beside two of her five husbands and most of her children, all of them, her victims.

15. *Life Magazine* reported at the time, how Rhonda especially enjoyed receiving get-well cards when her loved

ones were ill, and a torrent of lovely sympathy cards after
they died.

Emma

after *Under the Pure Air,* by Virginie Demont-Breton
(France) 1907

*"My whole life I was made to believe I was sick when I
wasn't..."*
Eminem, "Cleaning Out My Closet"

*"Factitious disorder imposed on another FDIA... first
named Munchausen Syndrome by Proxy... is a mental health
disorder in which a caregiver creates the appearance of
health problems in another person... the motive (is) most
commonly attributed to be a gain in attention or
sympathy...More than 90% of cases involve a person's
mother."*
Wikipedia

At first, the boy was easily seduced. The nurses were pretty
and had soft hands, and they smelled like soap and
raspberries. Henry needed their tenderness, too. They never
yelled the way Mama always did. And he noticed that the
more sick he was, the sweeter Mama became. She spent
more time fussing over him. She sat on his bed, stroking his
hair, rubbing his back. She let him soak in warm bubbles and
eat cupcakes.

Mother cried a lot, too, but that was nothing new, and it was
better than the yelling. Sometimes relatives and neighbours
stopped over and he would pretend to be asleep when she

opened his door. They all stood there looking at him, with her sniffling, and his uncle's arm steadying her. Big bursts of flowers kept coming, purple and yellow, with cards, and Mama hummed while she arranged them.

After awhile, Henry stopped liking the visits to the hospital. There were too many foul spoons of syrup and he had painful bruises wherever they put the needles in. He felt sleepy and sick to his stomach after the pills they made his swallow. He was bored and lonely and wanted to play with his friends. Mother would put red lotion that burned on the places the needles had been, then creams and bandages. He whimpered the whole while. She begged him to be strong for her.

One day he said he could be the strongest little boy in the whole wide world- would she watch him while he went into the backyard to climb the tree? It was bursting with fluffy flowers.

Mama slumped over, face in her hands, shaking while she sobbed. That was the day she told him the bad news. He had some kind of disease. Something rare. They didn't know what it was yet. Other little boys could play outside because they were healthy. But the germs in the yard or at school might make him really sick or even kill him.

Henry didn't want to die. He wanted to play hide and seek with the kids he saw on the street. He wanted to play road hockey with them, or go frog hunting at the lily pad pond near the hospital.

Henry felt scared and sad when Mama told him why he couldn't go to school. He asked if he had the same sickness his sister had had. Mama cried even more. She said no one was sure, because they didn't know what was wrong.

Henry was even smaller then and barely remembered Emma. Just the long days at the end there, days and nights of people coming and going with Tupperwares of triangled sandwiches and cut-up fruits. And the service at the cemetery, when he couldn't believe they were digging a hole in the dirt to put his sister in.

He looked out the window at the sunshine and the cherry tree. He hoped he wouldn't have to have more tests that made him vomit, or where they cut him open. He imagined shimmying up the knobby bark to find a perch. Swinging his legs from the big branch, shaking the blooms into the sky like a summer snow-globe. Watching the petals fall back to earth to cover her.

Farewell

after *Mother and Child,* by Egon Schiele (Austria) 1914

Your daughter, how she carries your mean hard heart, all
your darkness. A young woman, stranded here against the
sky. She can't help looking for you. She is talking to the
trees. Look at her shaking hands as she reads your eulogy.
Her face, and yours, the same river.

Gabble

after *Fat Flesh,* by Gabriela-Elena David (Romania) contemporary

The wide woman in the bumblebee pants struggles into the backseat of the Uber, dragging her bad leg in after her. Her husband patiently holds her purse and her cane, handing them to her and closing her door once she was inside, then circling the vehicle to climb in on the opposite side.

"Thank you for the ride, Rajesh!" Bill says, and asks the driver about his day as he helps Helen buckle in.

She squeezes his upper arm affectionately and he smiles. "Of course, dear. You good?" He admires how his wife continues to smile and laugh the way he has always known, even though the pain in her legs is severe. She can't teach anymore- it is not possible to run around after dozens of young children. But she is still that same colourful figure, the story-time teacher with the bright scarves and big glasses.

The driver is the talkative type, prattling on in a chirpy singsong voice about city affairs, so Bill asks him about his community and his favourite restaurants. Bill is always curious about others.

"Oh, excuse me, sir," Rajesh says and carries on but he talks quickly and is not easy to understand. It takes some time before they realize he is lecturing Helen about her considerable size. "Madame, you should not be asking about where to eat," he says, despite the fact that Bill was the one who asked. "You must make simple lifestyle changes and say no to the sweets. No excuses now. Dancing is very good exercise, very, very good. You must not take sodas or puddings so often, I'm afraid!" His unusually affable mannerisms make his tirade even more surreal. Bill and Helen are stunned, not able to believe their ears.

A lone tear slides from Helen's eye and she leaves it, hoping to avoid drawing Bill's attention to her upset by wiping it. He is so protective. She has of course talked to him about mourning the young and capable body she once inhabited. She wanted to give Bill her best, not this remaining wreckage. Every year she got thicker as her health deteriorated. She never expected to expand to twice the size and need help walking before fifty.

Rajesh is still talking. "Madame, be. sure to take many selections of plants and fishes and if you also make jogging every day, soon you will feel much better, believe me. You can enjoy whatever your husband eats! See how he is so slender and spry!"

Helen stiffens as her fury mounts. If she ate the same nightly barrels of candied cashews, double French fry orders dipped in gravy and mayonnaise, and cereals by the box, she would need a wheelbarrow for her stomach and breasts. Her shame is intense. Just last month, her doctor had recommended bariatric surgery, with prevention of diabetes in mind.

Helen pointed out that thirty years of thyroid dysfunction had made her fat, but wouldn't surgical trauma and deprivation further harm her slow metabolism? When the doctor scoffed, Helen asked her if it was true or false that half the people who got their stomachs stapled developed nerve damage in their hands and feet from nutritional malabsorption. "I see you've done your research already," the doctor huffed.

Helen feels Bill shifting from his gregarious and laid-back temperament into another. But this time, she beats him to it.

"You don't know anything about me," she says to the driver. "I can't dance… because I'm fucking *handicapped*. I had surgery on my leg and they made a mistake, so now I can barely use it. I was bed-ridden for two years. I would love to dance. Instead I scream from the pain if I use my leg too much."

"Oh, Madame, I am very sorry," the driver interjects, waving a hand nervously. "I did not mean to offend."

But Helen was just getting started. "Yes, you did," she continues. "You think you know best, even about a stranger's life. You feel superior to all of us fat miserable slobs. But you don't know shit!"

Bill reaches for her hand and pats it. "Oh, there's more," Helen says. "I'm also recovering from cancer, Mr. Driver. And I'm going to go out on a limb right now and bet that you, too, will know the joy one day. No matter how much fish you eat or if you're a vegetarian, or if you cook with turmeric or drink vats of green tea! You will, according to the odds, experience its ravages. Do you know what they give you when they inject you with the toxic sludge that they hope kills the cancer? Steroids. They fatten you up like a pig before the slaughter."

They arrive home before Bill can get a word in edgewise and long before Helen is finished saying what she has to say. Fuming, she flings the door open, and after the painful and difficult task of extricating herself from the car, she slams the door so hard that the whole vehicle shudders.

Bill comes behind her, dutifully carrying her purse. What did she do to deserve a loving soul like his?

She shuffles toward the entrance, flinching with each painful step. She feels ridiculous now in the flowing yellow striped palazzos that she wore to the BBQ at Bill's brother's house. She had felt fun and festive when getting ready, but now in her embarrassment and her rage she feels like a giant yellowjacket.

She thinks about the years just before the surgery went wrong, long afternoons of yoga and mineral water and bike rides with Bill along the river. Sometimes after those beautiful miles together, she would surprise him by climbing up top and taking the reins, feeling, for a few moments, perfect and whole and loved, forgetting everything else.

Merry and Bright

after *Old Age Home,* by Wilhelm Heinisch (Germany) 1950

Mother is in the bingo hallway with a dauber in each hand and a collage of cards in front of her. She can't really see them, she can't really hear the numbers. But it's something more than staring at the ceiling.

The residents are all decked out in Santa hats. Some of them are slumped back, slack-jawed, snoring. An orderly is pushing a trolley of hot chocolate in Styrofoam cups, distributing them to anyone who is awake.

"It's about time you came to see me," Mother barks when she registers our presence. I tense up instantly, but Jim touches my shoulder gently, reminding me I promised to do my best. "Good to see you, Mom," I say, giving her a big hug. I hand her a massive gift bag with an oversize plush basset hound inside. Jim's friend's wife was knitting elf outfits for pets and we got one for the toy. I can tell Mother loves him, because she drops a dauber on the floor in the scramble to free him from the wrapping. She told us as often as she could that she missed her dogs much more than she missed her kids, or grandkids. Then she wondered why they didn't make much of an effort to see her.

The stuffed animal was both my middle finger and a gesture of love for a lonely and bitter old woman. Love, and pity.

"Ah, yes, I see," Mother says, after the initial rush of her gift wears off. "You're doing your duties of visitation then," she rasps. "But you aren't planning to take me home for turkey dinner, are you? You've got everyone coming but me, yes?"

It is futile to remind her that she needs an orderly to help her into a van, and then she needs facilities equipped for wheelchairs, and that she has a three-inch gash across her jaw from the fall a few days past when she insisted on getting out of bed herself. "Don't kid yourself," she had hissed the last time I tried to explain these things. "That's what they tell you. I'm as spry as I've ever been."

"Yes, Mom, the kids are coming for Christmas." I can't blame her for hating it here, of course. And worse than anything, that feeling of being left out.

Maria shuffles over. She's sweet on Jim and comes to say hello whenever we visit. I wonder each time if Maria is as sweet as she seems, or if she is mean like Mother. She holds out a crooked hand to me, and then to Jim. "Merry Christmas, Maria," Jim booms. Maria beams.

"That woman throws herself at every man who walks in here," Mother says. It's a bit rich coming from the same mouth that propositioned him, way back when we were dating and a few times much later, too. "Give an old lady something to remember you by," was one choice request.

Jim is unfazed. He pulls out a batch of almond snowballs and sugar cookies shaped like candy canes. "I baked these myself, Mom," he says, popping one into his mouth and choosing one of each, placing them on a green and red napkin in front of her. She gives him a dirty look when he hands Maria the same selection. "Well, deck the bloody halls," she mumbles. But she digs in with gusto.

"Don't let her steal your spirit," Jim says as he drives us home. "Your mom has never been happy. That's her choice, but it doesn't have to be yours."

Jim is a goofy and kind soul. I'm lucky. On our first Christmas together, he pinned several dozen mistletoe balls to the ceiling, a few in every room. "I just want to keep on kissing you and kissing you," he explained.

A few tears escape. I can't help it. A bit of guilt over Mother's misery. A bit of fear I'll be there one day, too. A lifetime of carrying her bitterness.

Jim passes me a handful of wadded up tissues from his pocket. They smell like cherry Halls.

It starts snowing, big wet sploshes of white. Jim clicks the windshield wipers on. He fiddles with the car radio to find some festive tunes. When we hear the Jacksons singing, "I saw Mommy kissing Santa Claus…underneath the mistletoe last night…" we break into giggles, laughing all the way home.

Southern Soul

after *Lucinda Williams,* by Ron Olson (USA) contemporary

"If we live in a world without tears, how would scars find skin…how would broken find the bones?"
Lucinda Williams, "World Without Tears"

Lucy. Lean, all tooth, tough, but topsy turvy. The summer of seventeen. Blue jeans and silver rings and a guitar that was heavier than she was. The blistering air was hot with smog and pork and mango. Her favourite cantina is loud and humid. She takes a shot of tequila blanco before a cerveza.

She writes her own songs. But the hard-living men drinking here have soft hearts and hang on to her every word. They are men who spend all day fixing roofs or pouring concrete. They are missing teeth and missing fingers and they smoke and smoke. And they want to hear the American. She's shy, she's young, but she already knows she's got something, and they know it too.

After a few shots, she clambers onto the little stage and starts strumming. Even the pirate at the pool table stops his stroke and turns to listen. *Girl's got balls,* he says to his opponent. Her voice is raw and real. Small soul spilling open.

**

Girl from the south. Her father was a poet, put words in her blood. He was a teacher, Texas, Louisiana, Mexico City. Her jeans were barely filling out, and she was banging out the blues from bayou to zocalo.

**

Oh, there have been motorcycles and the men who rode them. Lucy straddles both sides of the highway. The holy, hollow halls where thin-haired bony tweed men with expensive certificates spout Pound and stir up trouble with the girls who iron their hair. And the road, with the roadies, and the juke boxes and the drums, and the sweaty men in leather, and the booze.

**

And now, suddenly, seventy. Her right side vanished in a stroke of midnight. She learns to speak again. Keeps writing, longhand, pencil, with an eraser. The songs keep coming. Her one arm hangs helpless against her denim hip. But she's still got the other.

**

"I didn't expect the stroke; there were no warning signs. I was real tired…I just didn't feel I could stand up."
Lucinda Williams, *Vanity Fair*
**

They say that when you get old, your memory gets rusty.

Lucy feels differently. She remembers everything.

**

Oh, there was nothing to stop her singing. Trends came and went. She never blinked. Just kept doing what she did. Just kept doing what she wanted.

There were big stars smattering the firmaments, and the pavement, anywhere she went. And she just kept on going.

There were poets, sweet and sensitive, and others, harder, mean. There was one that she loved, the one who put a bullet in his mouth, when another girlfriend found out about his wife.

Dry those tears, buttercup, Lucy said to the woman in the mirror. And on she went, writing, singing, slinging that guitar. One foot in front of the other.

**

"I don't want nothing, if I have to fake it."
Lucinda Williams, "I Lost It"

**

Alligators, cigarettes. Nacogdoches, Mississippi. Buses in the night through Alabama and Tennessee. Gas station coffee, Navajo turquoise, red wine. No way of stopping how those rivers of stories turn into songs.

**

The artist. The dark horse.

**

Where do the decades go? Where does the sun set when the swamps seep over the cities? When the rains keep pouring and the floods keep coming and the years keep going by?

The Desert Apothecary

after *Cerro Pedernal, viewed from Ghost Ranch,* by Georgia O'Keeffe (USA) 1941

There were two things Sadie loved more than her corner perch of the bar: smoking, and turquoise. She was a wizened, spindly thing, brackish and leathery, draped in ropes and chunks of sky-blue stones and silver that were heavier than she was.

Legend held she'd been quite a beauty back in the day and had traded that beauty freely to tourists and politicians for choice pieces by famed Navajo silver artisans.

If you asked her up front about the veracity of such stories, she would flash her wobbly teeth at you and rasp out a retort about it being a good investment.

Other local lore told she'd long ago had a husband and a son, both of them muckers and blasters over in Bisbee, both of them long dead from sick lungs.

When a bored city slicker in search of rustic and authentic living moved in and re-opened an old miner's drinking hole, Sadie was already an institution. That was in 1988. It was a desert town long emptied of even its ghosts by then, but city refugees from both coasts were starting to come to the area for their second lives, failed actresses from Hollywood and jaded art gallerists from New York, driven out by the impossible rents. The old crumbling tavern had been nailed shut for decades, but the first day it was dusted off and christened the Apothecary, Sadie was there, and she had never left.

The new incarnation of the Apothecary had a ridiculous menu of refreshments like orange blossom whisky and coffee vodka and craft beers infused with bergamot and raspberries. These appealed to the new kids and to the travellers, but most people, Sadie included, still ordered Old Overholt rye. A few fingers, neat, with ice on the side.

Sadie liked to roll American Spirit tobacco into cigarettes and gladly shared them with anyone who asked. You could follow her outside to puff away on top of a heap of old tires. You could smoke for hours, dazzled by the endless rippling scape of red rocks and blue above, broken by nothing for miles but the sculptural spines and pleats of the saguaro statues in the sand.

Sadie liked to tell you about her favourite ornaments, show you how her massive Zuni crucifix was turquoise on one side and red coral on the other, just like the world in front of you.

If she talked too long, she would start coughing and you'd worry she might never stop. Should her companions be persons of poor taste and point out the perils of her steady diet of whisky and cigarettes, Sadie would correct you kindly. Her tobacco was organic. The holes in her lungs and her kidneys were from the white man's poisons, same as her own men, centuries of soil saturated with uranium and arsenic from the greedy mines. And then she would shrug. Maybe it was all just the price of beauty and art, she'd say.

She would show you another treasure, a cluster ring of creamy moon green stones, longer than her finger. Palomino turquoise, she'd tell you, from the mines in neighbouring Nevada. These ones are like bodyguards, healer stones, protectors.

When she started coughing again, as if she was splitting open from the inside, you'd worry she might break. But you'd be wrong.

Uncle Satan

after El Tio effigy sculptures (Cerro Rico, Bolivia) past and contemporary

1. The devil is hung like a horse. Ramrod red, his prick protrudes between gangly splayed legs in rubber boots. He is festooned in rainbow ribbons. His effigy lurks in every mineshaft alcove under Cerro Rico. His sinister grin is stuffed with cigarettes. Lord of the Underworld, the devil squats on his throne of Puro empties.

2. *El Tio* loves beer and rubbing alcohol, but they're not his libation of choice. He is bloodthirsty. At the annual Carnaval, the Oruro and Potosi locals feast and dance with the devil. A big brass band makes merry as blindfolded llamas are wheeled in for slaughter. The yatiri, the witchdoctor, passes out knives. Miners brush their cheeks with llama blood. The rest is all for Uncle, so that he will be satiated and spare the workers their own.

3. It is not enough: El Tio wiggles filthy fingers. He wants more. The villagers rip *el corazon* from the beasts and kiss them, then offer them to Uncle. He likes his hearts still beating.

4. All night, there will be music and fires and drinking until obliteration. There will be saltenas, and tripe with peanut sauce, and llama charque and spicy llajua. There will be rostro asado, a whole sheep's head tenderized with a miner's blow torch.

5. The white ribbon clouds, the red dust roads. All is silent when the festival ends. Eternity spills from these barren hills, stretching ahead as dry and fruitless as the silver veins inside, below. Every miner dreams of that lucky strike. But after five centuries and 60 000 tons of silver excavation, only scraps remain.

6. Supay is an ancient god of the mines of the Andes in Inca and Quechua history. He was lord of the hills and lord of death long before the arrival of the Catholic devil. Supay is Uncle, or Uncle's helper, or manifest through Uncle, or Uncle's friend. Uncle is local to Cerro Rico, syncretized by Supay and Satan.

7. A little lead, a bit of zinc and tin. All that's left. Nearby Potosi, once the thriving Imperial City, is a remote and dusty ghost town. It was the jewel of New Spain and the colonial empire. Now that the mines are nearly bereft, El Tio's mountain finally belongs to the indigenous people of Bolivia. It is the burial ground for thousands of Brown and Black slaves. Many say the real devil is Spain.

8. A boy emerges from a crevice between rocks, pushing a wheelbarrow. Blistered hands, sandals tied by twine. Countless children work inside. The mountain that eats men, they say, men, and boys. Tattered rope ladders drop thirty feet into caverns too narrow for small men to crawl. Shafts crumble under dynamite and time. Miners crawl for miles on hands and knees. There are tunnels that lead where no one knows, where men disappear into the darkness.

9. The women from the villages wear long and layered prairie skirts and bowler hats. They bring booze, and coca leaves, water, empanadas, anticuchos. They pray to the Virgin of the Tunnels. They wait for their men and boys.

10. The worst way to die happens to all who survive the devil inside. *Silicosis.* Inhaling crystalline silica ravages the alveoli and slowly chokes a man to death. Those who evade collapses, explosions, rickets, starvation, injury, alcohol poisoning, and suffocation, will be dead from silicosis before they hit forty.

11. There are few statues or images of El Tio anywhere else. Only at Carnaval is the devil invited outside, when the annual dramas of good and evil involve him. Tourists take photos, but believers do not invite him outside on to God's land. The mines are the Uncle's realm. The villagers respect his kingdom. They pay the rent. They give the devil his due. They believe, because hell is real.

Vespertine

after *Moon Over Harbour,* by Edward Mitchell Bannister
(USA, b. Canada) 1868

She was a crepuscular creature, always, as much a part of the
gloaming as the crab-plovers and fireflies. After she got sick,
he would look for her, knew she'd be wandering the woods
with the nightjars and the rising moon, or rowing in the thin
weeds. He was still trying to find her. He followed her in the
shallows towards the oyster reefs. The humidity now was
close and dark above the brackish water. In the twilight bay,
she was out past the lighthouse, and finally, disappearing.
The vespertine world was closest to the other worlds, she
always told him.

Toilet Humour

after *Fountain,* by Marcel Duchamp (France) 1917

After the plumber pulled her spare eyeglasses out of the toilet with a drain snake, Abbie was surprised by a text inviting her to the new taco café in her neighbourhood. He used more quotation marks than words. *No worries if not!!!!! Hope it's okay to ask!!!!*

Abbie had noticed how the plumber's eyes were crinkly and warm when he laughed, and that his fingers were slender and long like a pianist's. Still, he'd literally been up to the elbow in her shit just half an hour before. She tried being nonchalant, cracking a few jokes. "So that's where those went," she said, laughing out loud while inside she felt sick with shame.

Mario was just doing his job, of course, and people's bathrooms were all in a day's work. She cracked a few lowbrow jokes he must have heard a million times, but he found her funny even so. While he examined her toilet, he made small talk about how he loved his job. He'd been stuck in an office, imprisoned "inside gray slacks" his whole life, until he was let go during the pandemic. His uncle gave him a stop-gap job and he found he loved wearing jeans and fixing faucets.

When Abbie confessed being squeamish about drain slime and bodily wastes, he said, "Yeah? Well, that's the kind of shit that washes off."

Abbie thought he looked like Ignacio from *Nacho Libre*, and that was how the subject of the taco shop first came up. The cult comedy was a guilty pleasure they shared, and then Mario mentioned a few comedians he found hilarious. He asked Abbie if she'd ever done stand-up. "I'm a veterinary nurse," she said, taken aback. After she said it, she wondered why the bodily fluids of her sick animals never bothered her.

"Well, I think you're really funny," the plumber told her. Abbie didn't mention her library files of Eugene Levy and Jack Black bits, or how she went alone to the Hell Hole to listen to open mic night. After she'd read *All Creatures Great and Small* she'd thought about getting up and doing some bits about the funny moments with dogs and ferrets at the animal hospital.

She didn't mention, either, her cursed litany of chronic diseases, and how most of her life revolved around various treatments, wraps and garments, swelling and pus and other disgusting things. He must have noticed that she staggered painfully because her one leg was twice the size of the other and that her face and arms were puffy. She was married once, but her husband wanted to do interesting things like travel, and she couldn't really risk flying or go anywhere without her edema pump, which cost thousands of dollars and several hours a day and took all the fun out of life.

Abbie had been gung-ho about being positive even after the divorce. She had even decided to try dating women. She had enjoyed the experience, but whoever said women were less concerned about appearances was lying.

Still, Abbie understood. She could lift up her stomach and put it into the bathroom sink, so it was tricky to get to the good bits. One night she sprang a leak and the rank fluids stuck inside her soiled someone else's sheets. Abbie was mortified by the revulsion on her girlfriend's face. After that, she stopped trying to explain lymphedema to anyone, and saved her affection for kittens and wounded dogs.

So she didn't return the plumber's text at first. While she was pumping her fluids that evening, she thought about what it might be like to simply go for Mexican food with a person who found her funny. In the morning, as she was pulling on her compression gear and work scrubs, she saw another text from Mario.

Is that an I'm shy, or attached, sorry?????? Or is that a get that corn outta my face!!!!!!!!!!!

Abbie found herself singing to her twin marmalade felines, Steve and Martin, as she set them up with food and water for the day. She was amused by the plumber's roasted corn reference from the *Nacho Libre* movie. It would be good- *real good-* to watch the film with a like-minded friend.

After her swim that night, she felt a surge of impulse and shot back, *Thursday at 7?*

She was pleasantly surprised to find Mario patient and helpful as she struggled in and out of his truck, and then again to find scrumptious tacos with chile-marinated meats and salsas, and lime, on real tortillas. "Mucho autentico!!!" Mario said, lifting his cerveza to clink with her *agua de*

Jamaica. There was more nervous small talk about movies. They discovered that they both loved Steve Carrell and that both named George as their favourite Seinfeld character.

"Look, I'm pretty rusty at this," Abbie said. "I haven't dated for years because of…" She tried to find the right words. "Because of…my illness." Best to be direct. "It takes up a lot of my time and energy. I was flattered by your invitation, and what can I say, you're a dead ringer for my favourite luchador. But I'm not sure where I'm at, or where you're at, right?"

"I'm not sure either," Mario said. "I wanted to get to know you better and took a chance. There was too much synchronicity not to bother. I enjoyed talking with you. And besides, I have a thing for orange cats." He rifled on his phone screen, then brought up some photos. "This is Mackinaw," he said, grinning widely.

After awhile, he said, "It must be so painful and frustrating. I hope you'll tell me more about it sometime so I can understand." The nervous exclamation marks were gone.

She would tell him more. But she wanted to know about him, too. Kids, alimony, a brother in prison, a religious conversion, a mother with dementia… What kind of shit had he gone through? It could be anything.

"You first," she said.

The Monday Jar

after *Natura Morta,* by Giorgio Morandi (Italy) 1957

The jar was plain enough, standing out from the others for its lack of adornment. The rest were elaborate patterned enamel swirls and flowers, old Turkish treasures with sensual, curved necklines and flared spouts. Another had glass as light as a bird's skeleton, exquisitely etched by a master hand. The shopkeeper had an eye, to be sure, but the one that caught her attention was sturdy and serviceable, off-white, ceramic, with a mouth wide enough for her hand.

Penny loved rifling through junk shops for curious objects and beautiful ornaments. When she pulled into the plaza, it was the medical mart she was after. Ted needed special socks for his swollen ankles, and new rubber tips for his cane. A neighbour had suggested this place for its impressive selection. Penny couldn't help noticing the collectibles corner at the end of the strip, a welcome distraction after rows of hemorrhoid donuts and bandages. Today she passed over the allure of yesterday's crackling leather-bound hymn collections, and jaunty fascinator millinery. She reached for the simplest vase.

Ten bucks. Perfect.

"You sure about this one?" asked the fellow at the front. There was something peculiar about his affect, and his angles, everything sharp and jittery.

"I am," Penny said. She waited for his upsell speech. The enamel vases were no doubt more than $100. He took her money, but he hesitated then. "This jar comes with an apparent curse," he said. "I could show you a nice milk jug. Is it for flowers?"

Penny shrugged off her annoyance. Antique people were all a little odd and many had strange beliefs. They lived in the past, after all, a world of folklore and things half-known, and it was part of the enchantment you were seeking when you bought old things. Today's assembly line stuff did not have the same spirits and stories.

"What kind of curse?" she asked. She couldn't help herself. If she was buying a genie with her bottle, all the better, she thought. But this particular jug was not so exotic and not very old. It was probably made in a small factory a state or two away, and just a few decades ago.

"I do not know the nature of the curse," the thin man said. "But this jar is always returned to us. We are of course happy to refund our unsatisfactory products …" He tapped with sharp fingers a notice for ten day returns. "However, the small expense doesn't seem to be the problem here."

"Well, what *is* the problem?" Penny asked.

"We aren't sure," the man said gravely. "The last several owners have all said this jar ruined their life."

"I'll take that chance," she said lightly, stuffing the jug into bag with Ted's new socks.

Driving home, she felt a bit of excitement. She had already talked to Ted about the Monday Jar. It was something from a talk show she had seen, a concept for couples designed to "invite intimacy back into your marriage." The idea was fairly straightforward. You put your fantasies and fun ideas on little pieces of paper. Every Monday, you randomly pulled one from the jar. And that week, you found ways and time to bring the fantasy to life, together.

Ted thought the Monday Jar sounded a bit like dirty dice, those corny smut novelties you rolled that might land on "kiss" and "toes." But he was still game. Like Penny, he wondered where the years had gone and how they had both grown soft and veiny around the edges. Ted managed diabetes and Penny shared the woes of his neuropathy, hers a gift from the chemotherapy she survived. Pleasure wasn't often on their minds, so he thought that a saucy game that could get them naked more often wasn't a bad idea.

Being more playful together appealed to Penny, too. They had weathered the temptations and monotonies of married love rather nicely, when so many couples, if they stayed together at all, never made love, and acted so bitterly towards each other. She and Ted could be sad or frustrated like anyone else, but they worked to cherish each other rather than grow into enemies. Sex was of course different and less frequent than when they were newlyweds, and modified by their various aches and woes, but they still found ways to connect and love.

The first few weeks were promising. The tab that Ted pulled from the jar put a twinkle in his eye. They were more touchy feely than usual after that. The Monday after Penny pulled a paper out, they both braved the sex toy supermarket, laughing together while feeling all kinds of buzzing plastic and gooey unguents. They took delight over being the oldest couple in those glossy aisles.

It was tough to pinpoint when things started to disintegrate in the rush of lust and laughter, or when their chummy closeness started to change. But along the way, they started to grow ill at ease. Penny felt weirdly vulnerable that a few of her filthiest fantasies were floating in the Monday Jar, ready to surface in the light of day by chance selection. She felt sick one week to discover a trick she'd been using for years on Ted was all wrong. This time, she burst into tears when she read the random Monday paper. Ted got angry because Penny had insisted they be honest and uncensored when they started this part of their erotic journey. He didn't like feeling judged when he'd been so willing to entertain her unexpected needs.

"Trouble in paradise?" the man at the collectibles corner asked. He did not seem surprised to see her. He pointed at the ten day returns sign. "I don't want a refund," Penny assured him. "We just don't want the jar. Please take it." The man nodded as he unwrapped it.

"You think you know someone," Penny said, mostly to herself, as she was leaving.

The Man in the Golden Mask

after *The Last Fiesta,* by Chris Parks (USA) contemporary

"No one would have taken me seriously as a wrestler had they known I was a priest."
Fray Tormenta

Sergio Gutiérrez Benitez, Cieneguillas, Mexico. Population 200. Seventeenth of eighteen mouths to feed. They do their best, but his father is a lowly *carbonero,* a charcoal peddler, who travels to sell his wares. The closest town is fourteen hours away by donkey.

When the young boy's uncles are murdered by banditos- or is it a family feud?- the whole clan makes their way to the big city. The brothers grow up in the slums of Mexico City, in the Tres Estellos barrio under Tepeyac Hill. The shrine of Guadalupe is where Mary first appeared in a blue-starred mantle to a poor shepherd, speaking softly in Nahuatl, his own Aztec language: *"¿No estoy yo aquí que soy tu madre?"* *("Am I not here, I who am your mother?")*

Sergio is a gang member by the tender age of ten. He takes work at a pencil factory, and sells popsicles at the circus. But punching and brawling are natural to him. He is constantly fighting, proudly collecting scars from every battle. He has been stabbed like a turkey Christmas carcass. He has been shot. He has been smashed with broken bottles. Sergio smokes; he drinks himself blind from the roadside buckets of pulque. He takes the pills, the powders, the pipes, and the needles.

Perhaps Sergio's story is the same story as every luchador. Mexican wrestling is a surreal theatre of men in cosplay beating the shit out of each other. It is performance art, and a gladiator sport, both. It is a ritual enactment of the battle of good and evil. It is wildly popular throughout the country. Audience members have their favourite players in the drama. The arena gives glamour and glory to the masked men, who may otherwise have a terrible existence. Every little kid wants to grow up to be a luchador fighter. For those entrenched in violence and poverty, it is a way out, a way of being or becoming something else, a glimmer of grandeur.

Sergio reads the same comic books and watches the same movies as other boys his age. He is a teenager when he sees the films *El Señor Tormenta* and *Tormenta En El Ring* (*Mr. Storm, Storm in the Ring*). Sergio dreams about becoming a luchador. He also dreams of a bigger fight, a fight for God, becoming a priest to help the children who have been forgotten. Both of the movies were about a hero with a double life- a luchador who is secretly a priest, or a priest who is secretly a luchador. The hero uses his rewards to help orphans. It is exactly the kind of story that Jack Black will tell later, from a comedy perspective. By then, because of Sergio, it will be based on a true story.

When Sergio is barely twenty, his friend is murdered in the mayhem of it all. He is the one accused, but he manages to prove his alibi, a cantina far away from the scene of the crime.

But now he wants out. He walks into a church, and he prays.

He is tossed away. He tries again. Eventually he lands in a rehab in Tlalpan. When he joins a seminary, he can't help throwing punches. "How are you going to break a wild colt from night to morning?" Sergio asks *Vice Magazine* in retrospect, at age 70.

He is determined to become a priest, and struggles against the demons that have him in their grip. He is sent to Navarra and to Rome, and learns psychology, theology, philosophy. He is especially interested in sociology and psychology and studies to understand juvenile delinquency.

He becomes a priest with the Order of Poor Clerics Regular of the Mother of God of the Pious Schools. He is a fighter through and through, in every way.

His first post is in Veracruz, the Gulf's port city, loved by pelicans and by pirates. Sergio's parish is filled with the least of these, *"drogadictos, prostitutas, y delincuentes."* Some ruffians taunt him, tempt him to blows. They say they can't trust someone who doesn't fight.

This is the beginning of the long secret, the Man in the Golden Mask. Father Sergio understands he has been called by the Almighty to a most unusual task, to becoming the legendary Storm in the ring.

By day, he feeds the hungry, and gives the Bread of Life to hungry souls. By night, he wrestles under the cover of a red and gold satin mask. He will wear it in his cameo later, in the movie *Nacho Libre*.

Father Storm begins collecting destitute and damaged children. He does not abandon them when he moves, but rather takes them along when his priestly duties change. He grows his roving orphanage through the funds he earns as a clandestine luchador. He takes on thousands of fights in his homemade masks. "Gold is for the Divine. Red is for the blood I shed for His children."

One day, when the cat is long out of the bag, he christens the orphanage "La Casa Hogar de los Cachorros de Fray Tormenta" – that is, "the House and Home of Fray Tormenta's Puppies."

Today, Sergio is nearly 80. Though he retired from the ring more than 20 years ago, he occasionally makes guest appearances. He continues to work with his charity for underprivileged children, because he will always be one of them. He trains them in grapples, rolls, and dives, because they dream of wrestling. But he also teaches them reading, writing, and arithmetic. He feeds them. He gives them medical attention. Fray Tormenta has raised over 2000 children.

Today Father Benitez still does the mass in his Texcoco parish, and he does it wearing a cape, Spandex and the famous golden masks. Only in Mexico!

Truth is stranger than fiction, as anyone who's read the Good
Book knows.

Sepsis

after *The Artist's Father in his Sickbed,* by Lovis Corinth
(Germany) 1888

Vinegar and bleach and still, under everything, the vague
stink, medicinal and fecal, always there on the outskirts. He
wonders why these institutions never open the damn
windows. The sick and dying are not in prison, after all. Let
some fresh air into the space.

His daughter has adopted the inside voice that the nurses and
technicians always use. Kind, impersonal, sweet, but at
arm's length. Even the brochures that explain treatment
protocols or side effects are dumbed down, as if the only
people getting cancer are all in kindergarten.

Red daubs at his drool, distressed that Liz has to see him this
way. Her singsong consolations make it worse. *Don't worry,
Dad.* Don't worry! As if he has no dignity left to save. *It's
okay, Dad. It's okay.* Is it really? When did it come to this, a
girl being okay with her father's life coming to its ending?

Red feels the warm spread of urine releasing into his diaper
just as he starts floating in space. He wants to hang onto his
daughter's cooing murmurs. But he's in and out. It could be
the drugs, all these dreams. There are enough pills already,
but with the infection now, there are more. A dozen
altogether? No idea now, he simply opens his mouth like a
baby bird and swallows on command. And right now, he is
deep inside the liminal with all his ex-wives and a weird and

stark landscape covered in Astroturf and no damned thing from the land of the truly living.

When he comes back, she's gone. Of course. They always duck out when the almost dead are sleeping. They make a run for it. Sleep never lasts long. They weave here and there, back and forth, in and out. It's a lonely borderland. No one wants to wait. What if he came back in, and found himself still holding her hand, saw her in the corner with her laptop fired up, working? And if instead of saying Okay, Dad, I'll just let you rest, and disappearing, she said, I'm here, Dad, just filling in the boxes I need to for Thursday's deadline. I'm not going anywhere.

A nurse comes into the room, scurrying in the half light to check his IV and get out of there before he stirs. I'm awake, he says dully. How do you ask for company? How do you say you're afraid, or ask someone else to take on your pain? You can't. Not really. It's the terrible irony. Where you are going, no one can accompany you now, but everyone will go there.

Nightmares

after *Untitled (Red, Orange, Orange on Red),* by Mark Rothko (USA, b. Latvia) 1962

When Mother was finally slipping from this world to the next one, she told me that in the long night before, she had not seen the white tunnel but rather red fire. She saw Jesus, but his back was turned. And oh, how she missed her mother and her father, and oh, how we cried together there in those throes of everything, at all the cutting away at the roots.

Wasabi

after *Doctor Dissecting His Own Limb,* artist not known
(Belgium) c. 1715

Brian had never known Jackie to be a sore loser, but tonight
she was in a bit of a huff. They'd lost two rounds of Catan at
their monthly game Friday with friends. Jackie sat moodily
in the Uber with her arms crossed, looking out the window.

"I don't want to go anymore," she said finally.

Brian suggested they play Hearts or Poker next time. Jackie
got pretty lucky at regular cards. "I don't care about that!"
she said. "I'm just tired of Brad and Nina. Nattering on all
night about the bloody elections. It's always the same crap."

Jackie had wanted to go to a series of plays put on by a local
church group, then a couple's cooking class. She had
suggested a late summer blues festival down by the wharf.
There was a burlesque event where the audience was
supposed to dress up, too, and a gem and jewelry expo at the
convention centre. There was a bourbon tasting thing. There
was a haunted hayride. But she was always out-voted, and
staying home to play Catan became a thing some years back.

At home, when she got out of the shower, Brian was half
asleep. She clicked the remote to her current show, *House of
Flowers,* an over-the-top dramedy about a Mexican family
who owned a flower shop and a drag queen cabaret. Jackie
had a big crush on the Diego character, the family's financial
adviser and the brother's older boyfriend. He was so

debonair in his tailored suits and had a yummy smattering of soft freckles and a gorgeous silver hair and beard.

After awhile, Jackie got out of bed and started digging around in the pantry for pretzels. She saw a dusty bottle of merlot, then located a corkscrew. What the hell, she thought. They had beautiful fishbowl glasses that had never been used. She poured half the bottle in, and went back to bed.

Just as the first gulps of wine coursed through her bloodstream, Juan Pablo as Diego entered the frame, leaping passionately on his beau. He kissed with desperation, and with his whole body. She wondered if Brian would ever kiss her like that again.

"Brian," she said, poking him conspiratorially. "Share this with me." He woke just long enough to register surprise because wine was usually for special occasions. But he'd never been bothered by her crushes on TV detectives or old movie sirens. "Is it Dr. House tonight?" he asked, and then he was asleep again.

Jackie turned back to Juan Pablo and Julian embracing. She Googled the actor and found incredible photos of him wearing a wasabi-coloured suit, then an apricot one. It was the same colour as the roses and bridesmaid dresses at her wedding. Juan Pablo's megawatt toothy smile gave her full body tingles. She swooned over a photo of him in his library, shelf after shelf of artist monographs, Giacometti, Marcel Duchamp, Rufino Tamayo. She couldn't believe it when she found out that Juan Pablo was straight in real life. He threw himself into his gay romantic role without restraint, holding nothing back.

But most shocking was learning the actor had recently lost a leg.

Jackie read an interview where he talked about living fully after a dark depression and an amputation. He'd suffered a sudden silent heart attack in his early forties, his body riddled with blood clots. She kept thinking about Juan Pablo's brush with death and his deliberate embrace of life.

Brian didn't understand whatever it was Jackie was going through. When he confided later to his brother that she was more amorous and adventurous than she'd ever been, that she was taking bubble baths and wearing perfume and ordering Champagne, Paul asked if it could be an affair. Brian panicked. He'd read an article once that suggested unexpected surges of lust in a long marriage could signify infidelity. It couldn't be, could it?

Things were definitely strange. Jackie had pulled out an old set of crutches from the storage room, relics of a college skiing mishap. She had a skimpy little nurse-style getup on. "I want you to be brave," she had whispered, then tethered Brian's hands to the bedposts with a tensor bandage.

Brian searched through their shared computer for clues. He wouldn't breach her privacy by snooping her mobile. He found nothing amiss, but was puzzled by a long stream of Spanish films and a desktop folder full of pictures of a gay Mexican actor with very white teeth.

When game night rolled around again, Jackie reminded him that she wasn't going to Brad and Nina's. She had other plans. There was a modern art talk at the museum she had signed up for.

"Are you going with someone?" he asked then, and she was taken aback by the trembling in his voice. "Oh, no, Brian, no, of course not!" She put her arms around him. She smelled like mango and vanilla and roses. It was intoxicating. "Of course there's no one else. I'm happy to go by myself since no one else is ever interested in anything."

Brian asked why she hadn't said anything. "I did," she said, "over and over." And she turned to the foyer mirror to put on her lipstick.

In that moment, he realized it was true. Then he thought about the pictures of the Mexican actor, sparkling beside a pool and some sculptural furniture in his pale yellow knits, lounging in flowing bathrobes with stacks of art books and old Aztec statues everywhere.

"Will *this* silver fox do for your date tonight?" he asked, pulling Jackie close. She broke into smiles. "Of course! I already chose you, you know. Long time ago."

Brian asked for a few minutes to change his shirt and to text the first ever cancellation to Brad and Nina.

On a whim, he also Googled for flowers, looking for her favourite, butterscotch roses. A dozen of them, so they'd be waiting for her when they came home.

Beautiful Stranger

after *You'd Look Good on the Dancefloor,* by Christy Powers
(USA) contemporary

for Dimos 1976-2002

I fell in love with a beautiful stranger…
I looked into your eyes
And my world came tumbling down
Madonna and William Orbit

After

The angry red welt first came to Harvey's attention during a
shave.

Linda could not put into words how or why she found her
husband's manscaping rituals so comforting. He seemed
more bald and more naked without his big round glasses, and
he resembled a deranged luchador with the thick spread of
icing around his mouth and nostrils. But the daily sight of it
filled up her heart. It could still kickstart the rest of her, too-
she loved running her fingers across his squeaky-clean jaw
after his rinse, or pressing his face against hers.

Not this time. Harvey never worried the way Linda did about
every little fluctuation of the body. He took in stride the
natural aches and pains of middle age and beyond. But he
realized it was at least a dozen times now that he had shaved
around what he first thought was just an ingrown hair,
nothing more than an inflamed follicle.

Now he wonders if he should get it checked out. "Honey," he calls, points to the bump. Linda nods, tells him she has restrained herself for weeks from hounding him about it. She has already been reading about basal cell carcinoma. A possibility, but it was probably something else. "We can visit the clinic and rule out the worst," she tells him.

Of course, he knows about Nikolas. It was a long time ago that Linda lost her best friend. She had been quite a free spirit back then. Harvey knew it was that loss that changed her. Made her harder, and more stable, too, determined. They'd named their first daughter Nikola in her friend's honour.

It will turn out later that the questionable bump is just a cherry angioma, and harmless.

"Best to be sure," Linda reiterates. "Carcinoma is very common. But I don't think it's that."

"I don't either," Harvey says. "But I'll make an appointment this morning."

Linda pulls him close again and breathes him in. Another twenty years of him won't be enough. She's grateful for every single one.

**

Before

Your head was cocked, reflecting on your reflection. You turned your baby face just so and just so to take it all in. I imagined you this way even when no one was looking. *Who's a pretty birdie now, Nikolas?* I thought, sidling up to you.

You squeaked a bit, and erupted into giggles. That wide grin, pure mirth.

The first little ripples of molly were tapping at the periphery. We kept laughing. You greased up your lips with something pale blue and sparkly, and we both pinned on fresh lashes from the dollar store, pretended they were mink and 24 karat gold.

You were dabbing and dabbing at an imaginary blemish with my coverup stick. But I could feel the underbelly of the beat beyond the door. It was rolling in, dark and deep, slow waves, hypnotic and transcendent. I wanted to dive into the dancefloor. "Come on, Nikolas!" I plucked at your second-hand silk.

The music broke just then, tumbling out of the night and surrounding us with epiphany. I could literally see sparks coming off of Madonna in the air. The ecstasy was just about to kick in hard.

And I feeeeeeeeeel … like I just got home….

"Fuck, look at this thing on my face," you said, yanking my kite back down to earth. You were always flawless, and even close-up, all I could see was a small pink spot. It wasn't even a zit. I'd never seen you with a blemish. "No one can see it," I assured you. "Not even you." We started laughing again.

"Fuck, girl, what if it's AIDS?" Your pitch now was a panicked squeal.

"Whatever, girl," I said. "You might be getting a pimple! It happens."

The siren song of trance was weaving its way into under beat. We were getting higher. You were still fixated on the blemish and I didn't want it to turn into a bad trip.

"It's got a blue tinge," you said. "Do you think it could be Kaposi's sarcoma?"

I pointed at my own purple pallor. "That's from the trippy lighting, sweetheart! Relax. Besides, I'm pretty sure KS is one of the last stages of AIDS, for fuck's sake." I put my arm around you. "Forget about it, sweetie," I said. "We'll see someone after. We'll get a doctor to rule it out. It's nothing, you'll see."

Five months later, you were dead.

**

Before Before

You were only that beautiful stranger for a few seconds. You found me daubing designer cologne onto my wrist at the department store counter, tried to sell me a hundred dollar bottle of Angel. I took a handful of the sampler swabs, said I would love to always smell like you.

We were inseparable after that. We ripped through boxes of cheap Chardonnay and went dancing every night. We shopped every sale and shared our closets. We bought huge fluffy robes and fuzzy bellbottoms at the thrift shop and lounged in bed watching soap operas. We practiced imitating Madonna and her dancers for hours and showed off our moves at fabulous nightclubs. We took a night class on literature together, fell in love with Tennessee Williams and Hart Crane. We would show up at library lectures or author readings, teetering precariously on stiletto boots and pink wine. Our friendship was eternal, invincible. You had a punk T-shirt that you hacked off at the midriff and bedazzled. *Live fast and die young.*

Mackerel

after *Untitled (The Nightmare Tree),* by Zdzislaw Beksinski
(Poland) before 2005

for Cormac McCarthy 1933-2023

The wells are thick with death, graveyard schools of fish
dried by the hell sun into rancid chewy jerky.

They can't risk it. The protein would put some meat on those
bones. But the poison could kill them. No.

They turn away. Distended bellies, growling bowels. The
stark white sun-lord looming overhead. No relief until the
earth starts to tilt toward night. And even then. The thick
humid ash hovering over everything will still be there.

They file past an orchard just as a gray moon starts its ascent.
The glorious fragrance of overripe apples. They move in,
pluck what's left of the fruits to distribute. He bites inside,
eager for water and sugar, but the red globes are long mealy
and returning to worm.

They lay out their tarps on the bed of rotten fruit. The stink
of dried fish on the downwind over the old orchard. They
suck the last liquid out of every available apple so they don't
die of thirst before dawn cracks and urges them on.

He is hardly a few dead trees away from the woman he once
wanted to marry, the one who got away from him before it
was the end of the world. He can hear her breathing in the
rank and humid darkness. He thinks for a moment that she

has whispered his name and he pauses in his mind for a second before disappearing. Deep inside his dreams he is swimming. The black water cooling his fever, the island cave springs of another life. The dream changes. He sees the woman atop a pirogue, strange pyre, floating from the mouth of the tunnel. Long mummified by the sweltering sun.

Morning comes. They go on.

Poison

The camp at the edge of the hospital is an eyesore and a dangerous maze. There are fecal landmines everywhere. Jane can't avoid it, unfortunately, because the camp is right by the doorway into the ward. Her cane strikes pavement, steadying her against the slippery spills of booze, before or after imbibement, and the dam of dirty needles.

She braces herself each week before treatment, but cannot avoid the disgust. How the city and the hospitals allow the squatters their squalor here is beyond her. It's not compassionate to the homeless, or the sick who need medical care, or the folks simply walking past to get to work.

Revulsion thickens on her tongue, settling into the thrush from the Docetaxel, already a yeasty swamp layered atop the tin can and rotten fruit flavours sticking to her palate. But inside the airless, windowless halls where people are supposed to heal, it grows still worse. The herds on the wards, all desperate and most dying. The occasional declaration of hope or uplifting prognosis is almost cruel against the backdrop of decay and demise. And the stink of it all- chlorohexidine, biohazardous liquids for their veins. The truth underneath it: shit, and death.

Today's slow drip comes with a cougher in the next pod and a rubbery egg salad sandwich in Saran Wrap, along with a plastic cup of ice chips. The cliché is true: it's a race to cheat the poisons, let them kill the cancer before they kill you. For

Jane, so far, so good, sort of. There are sores swelling inside her throat, and raw blisters between her buttocks; painful edema leaking from her blood vessels into her toes and ankles. Her bowels are intermittently frozen for days or exploding, sometimes soaking bright red streaks onto the paper. Her gums bleed, too. Her fingernails are pulling away from the flesh, and her skin is parched and cracking. Her sinuses are a fountain and there is fluid in her lungs. Her heart jumps all over the place, improvisational jazz over rhythmic pumping now the norm.

She can't sleep and she can't stay awake. Her muscles are too weak to pick up the cat or walk without resting every few steps. Menopause was instant, a decade too soon. Her urine is caustic. Her immune system is toast. And that lash-less rabbit stare.

The piece de resistance, of course, always- all those years of growing out her beautiful hair, fallen from her scalp in a weekend.

But what doesn't kill you makes you stronger. Jane's been dodging death all her life. Now, this, too. And this, too, shall pass, no?

When every last drop from the tub of toxins has been pushed into her body, Jane texts her ride and makes her way outside. At the traffic lights, one of the tent dwellers approaches. The woman's body is twitching with electricity, and her eyes are wild. Her greasy hand pushes into Jane's face, in petition, for money that isn't there.

No, sorry, Jane says, and it is what almost everyone says. No rote chirp of "have a nice day" from these crusty lips and bones. Instead, the junkie says, "Well, well, well, what a surprise. Little Miss Cancer, do you think you own the world?"

A mean one. Jane fights back tears, then fury. The entitlement! If only she could hand her medical bills over to the junkie! She imagines a phoenix rush of energy and power, a blazing swing at the enemy, striking her down for insolence and audacity. The adrenaline turns back to a thin wisp, an empty stream, before the light can change.

A long time ago, many years past, a friend said to her, "It's just unbelievable, these twelve step programs, how dare they compare addiction to illness? How do you think someone who actually has cancer feels when they hear that? It's disgusting." Jane hadn't thought about that for a very long time. But now she does.

She turns back to the hollow woman. "You don't know me," Jane says. "But I know you. I was you. Once."

The woman's scabby hands claw the air, and her cracked lips are a gash of venom at the idea. But Jane continues. "I made it, then. And maybe I'll make it this time, too. Will you?"

The light finally changes. The junkie doesn't answer, and doesn't follow her, but turns her dirty hands upward at the next pedestrian prey. Unlikely, Jane thinks, as she crosses slowly. Anything is possible, sure, but the chances the woman will clean up, survive, and thrive, are slim.

About the same chances as hers, she thinks, as she spots her friend waving by her car.

As they drive away, Jane thinks about the addict, wonders about her name. And then she moves on.

Crow Funeral

after Anguish, *by August Friedrich Schenck (Germany) 1878*

for Erika, with love

Driving fast. A big sky afternoon. The high sun is yellow and the tulips are yellow and the old truck is yellow. When Joni Mitchell chimes in from the dial radio, of course it's "Big Yellow Taxi" and Jess and Arrow laugh and their laughter runs along the vineyard roads like fluttering goldfinches.

So many crows. Arrow sees them first, startling, telling Jess to slow down. The tree in front of the Jakes's barn bowing low from the weight of them. They perch in clusters in the beech and hemlock trees that wind into the woods and stream down the way.

Jess pulls over, eyes wide, red mouth round. Some of the birds are hopping on the grass with jumpy movements in some kind of ceremonial dance. There are crows flying in, taking their place on branch or below or on the walls of an old stone well.

They watch for a few minutes, silent, solemn. Thinking, watching. Something elemental, primordial, about all those crows.

After a while, Arrow turns to her friend. "Jess," she says. Looks at her, looks down. "Have you ever seen a murder?"

*

Years later, and all the vines still covered in winter. Arrow's father. There, at the place of the crow funeral. Huddled in a copse of apple trees, knees up, head down, a butcher's knife slid to his hems and undone boots. Zigzac criss-cross wounds slashing both his wrists, a river of blood in the snow.

*

Arrow who knew all these things, the things that Jess did not, told her more about the crows after their drive. How what they had seen that afternoon was a corvid funeral.

How crows and other corvids like rooks and jackdaws gathered in mourning.

When these proud creatures found one of their family fallen, they cawed repeatedly until word spread and crows from all around gathered in masses to stand with and sing to their dead. Jess explains that the collective noun for a gathering of crows is a "murder."

The girls hadn't been close enough in their truck to see the dead bird, but Arrow was certain it wasn't another kind of crow picnic. Jess loved the poetry in Arrow's mind, the ways that words and symbols and all the things in the world belonged to her, how she could tell them and christen them in the telling. They would get under her skin, these things of sadness and marvel and beauty.

*

They'd always known each other. Since the days of rolling potato bugs and skipping ropes and knee band-aids. Saints.

Witches. Sisters or something, but different. Nothing could change that. Not this, not anything.

There had been so many storms. Sick horses and sick mothers and sick boys wanting strange things they couldn't understand. All those splinters of the daily strange working their weird fingers into young hearts. Jess took everything hard, she always had, always felt things through to her bones. Deeper.

Arrow found the words for her. She could open the Bible at random to a lamentation in the Psalms and read it like an age-old rite or an incantation. She marked meaningful situations spontaneously. Once when the mare was struggling to birth her foal and Jess couldn't stop crying, Arrow plucked wildflowers and scattered them in a circle when the moon rose over Willow Pond and everything turned out just fine.

*

Arrow's dad had been in a real bad state since the first shot and it got worse and worse after. They told him first it was just arthritis, but Arrow who sat up with him in the night knew that wasn't what it was. Then they said it was a virus, too far gone in his nerves and his neurons. He told them all his troubles started with the first shot of pandemic medicine, but they said that was a coincidence. At first he'd believed them and, like a lamb to the slaughter, he'd gone back for more. They dismissed his concerns as conspiracy theories. He became a pariah at work and in town. Eventually the doctors conceded what he already knew inside. Shrugged, hands up. Adverse effects were rare and tragic, and what could they do about it now?

*

Eric was a hockey dad, a spry kind of guy with an early shock of sterling silver hair and a flow of jittery energy that blazed until that first needle. He loved The Doors and Aerosmith and Hemingway. He loved big dogs and the blues. He kept all of Arrow's poems in a leather briefcase with a crimson ribbon tied through the handle.

*

Some nights, Arrow called Jess and asked her just to drive. They rolled and rolled through the winding road that followed the river. Janis Joplin or Joni or Sinead. One day Arrow gave her a bird skull necklace. So you'll always remember the crow funeral, she said, as if Jess would ever forget. Electroplated in copper. The delicate and ancient and fragile mystery of things.

*

Somewhere near the end of his pain, Arrow called crying. How her dad was halfway paralyzed and so very thin. The pain like a curse in his wrists and ankles and wherever else he was knit together. He'd given up working and driving and coaching kid's sports and trivia night at the pub a year past, and lived heaped across a futon in the corner, trying to keep his agony to himself. He was always cold as ice. The whole family beside themselves.

And Jess said, "Can he be helped into the pickup?" and came by and collected them, and they rode the miles in silence, three across, in and out of the orchards, into the morning.

*

When Arrow called again and said Eric's organs were shutting down and him only 56 and them doing nothing at all for his pain, Jess felt something swift and cold move through her. She called her friend again in the morning, and Arrow was crazy with grief, saying her dad had disappeared. He had taken the car during the night after a year or more of not driving, and no one could find him anywhere. "I'm looking for him, for the car, on every inch of the road," Arrow sobbed. And Jess said, "Oh, honey."

Somewhere inside she knew where he was and what they would find. "Oh, honey, no, no, stop driving, I'm coming. Oh, honey, you've got to let the police do the looking." Jess knew he'd gone to do what he was going to do where his wife and daughter wouldn't be the ones to find him.

A hoarse cry went up on the other end of the line, a staccato of cawing sobs like all the hope gone from her. Jess knew he had gone to where the crows had been. And that is where they found him.

*

And the years went by after that. Years full of sorrow and sickness, old and new, yes, but also gifts and blessings, like children and backyard ravens and friendship and summer marigolds. How so, when the whole world had stopped, and the injustice of a thing was so dark it could scarce be comprehended?

But this was the way of the world, wasn't it, still coming and going, again and again, even after it had ended. A terrible kind of magic. Now, the mornings full of asters and hummingbirds and fresh kittens.

But first, Jess watched her friend, so small and lonely, put together all the parts for the service. The order of grief. Proud to love her, proud of her strength. The medley of memories, the triangle sandwiches. The mourning playlist, Skip James and Charley Patton, and the fine bourbon, and how they all wore long and shiny silk and leather to gather, like black feathers.

Floating

after *Moonlight,* by Edvard Munch (Norway)1895

for Julee Cruise

In the late light, where the day dissolved to darkness. The deep still aqua velvet. She floated, face turned to the coming moon. The disappearing day a blazing apricot orb dipping at the horizon into the edge of the bay. She loved floating into the night. Untethered in the water. The pain that always anchored her was somewhere else for awhile. She let the cool water envelope and buoy her. The sounds of time in lulling ripples. The stars rose fast after the last serenade of the bullfrogs, when the nightjars began calling. And she kept floating, freely through the reeds and lily pads and out into the dark and diamond-dusted deep. One of these days, she would float right out to sea.

Little Miss Somebody

after *Self Portrait,* by Sarah Biffin (England) c. 1830s?

"Miss Somebody embroiders with her shoulder and elbow;
no need of hand and arms for the old purposes."
Hester Thrale Piozzi, 1818

The tiny portraits were exquisite. The collector polished his lorgnette and leaned in for a closer examination. The level of detail was astonishing. It was rare to see such delicacy in miniatures, some of them no larger than the button on his jacket. Bertram recognized the likeness of a duke and a baron. The other faces were not known to him, including one of a plump, curly haired beauty. While she was a fetching lass indeed, this miniature was not as skillfully rendered as the others. The subject appeared armless inside the puffs of her sleeves.

The label affixed to the display case claimed the artist was a woman. *Sarah Biffin.* Interesting. Bertram wondered which of these Miss Biffin works were for sale. His absolute passion was the building of his Kunstkammer. His collection was filled with art and artifacts from around the globe, and he particularly adored miniature works of outstanding skill.

Bertram did not share the familiar disdain of his colleagues for works by women. He understood that the hindrance of the fairer sex from the arts and sciences was not innate, but rather a societal and biological imposition on their advancement. Caring for children and the denial of education were just two of the biggest barriers facing them. Bertram was especially interested in rarities and curiosities. The more unusual and difficult to procure, the more personal value the pursuit of an acquisition held for him. It was not always easy to add creations by women to his cabinet. He felt that familiar rush of his pulse, thinking about choosing one of the intricate beauties to take home with him.

"Magnificent, aren't they?" A booming voice and a cloud of pipe smoke landed a little too close to Bertrand. He stepped back, nodding.

"Miss Biffin is a very talented painter from Somerset. Unfortunately, she is not here today for this exhibition, as she is working in Edinburgh at the moment. She is highly renowned and in much demand."

"Really?" Bertrand's interest was further piqued. He is a learned man and active in the spheres of art collectors, so he is puzzled that the name did not ring any bells for him.

"Oh, yes," said the gentleman. "Miss Biffin's trajectory is remarkable. You may know her better as Miss Somebody. His raised eyebrow gave wait for Bertrand's recognition. "Or, more crudely, The Mermaid of Margate. The Limbless Wonder."

A jolt of electricity ran up Bertrand's spine. There was a young woman, cruelly disfigured from birth, and just as cruelly paraded in a cage through the circus circuits. She had no arms and legs because of a condition called phocomelia. The sideshow posters exploited her presence with a depiction of a woman with stubby flippers instead of limbs. He had himself stood at her booth at Bartholomew's fair some years past, but he was not a man who tolerated crowds well, and did not wait in line to purchase her autograph. The handbills promised miraculous feats from Miss Somebody, only three feet tall, who could famously write, embroider, cut fabrics, and draw without hands. She used her shoulder stump and mouth.

"Yes, yes," said Mr. Boom. "Sarah Biffin has retired from the circus now. The Earl of Morton sponsored her education at the Royal Academy, and she now takes commissions from the Royal Family, as well as taking on students of her own."

Bertrand held up his lorgnette again to study the miniatures. Now he saw that the bust painting with the puffy sleeves was not imperfect after all, but was a self-portrait of Miss Biffin. He had to have it.

The asking price was reasonable. Bertrand inquired about arranging a meeting with Miss Biffin when she returned to London. Boom nodded, eager to secure the transaction. They moved towards the office to finalize necessary paperwork.

In his Wunderkammer later that afternoon, Bertrand poured himself a generous tumbler of brandy, and busied himself with arranging his cherished collection. He reverently caressed the anatomical Venus, removing the tiny ivory mass of intestines to dust them carefully with a feather. He rearranged the treasured carnelian amulets from ancient Egypt.

He wanted Miss Biffin's precious portrait to be perfectly displayed. A black velvet backdrop in a locked glass enclosure was ideal. But the box reminded him of the inhumane hutch she had endured, paraded from fair to fair, not unlike the fine specimens of taxidermy in this very room.

Still, there was no question that her work had to be behind lock and key. He opened the box of his fairest procurements and made space between an engraved sterling baby rattle and a pair of Qajar bird ear baubles. Miss Biffin's courage and determination were fine jewels indeed, and he wanted to show her the place of honour and respect that she deserved.

Nocturne

after Gertrude Abercrombie

The woman walks away from the pain and the noise. The path a trident fork of fates, each a silver stream splintering under the spherule moon. Where do we go when going nowhere? Anywhere but here. A copse of sleeping apple trees all that's left of the old orchard.

The Manny

after *With One Touch Her Spirit Soared*, by Nancy Willis (England) 1994

He was lean and khaki, like a grasshopper. Face flint and sharp, arms almost down to his knees. I needed someone who could carry me, and he could. "Look," he said, when he came in, "it is very bad for my family back home, I need this." I explained to him that the job was not caring for children, but for me. I was an artist who needed an assistant, sometimes with my work but mostly as a kind of nurse and janitor.

It wasn't easy work, and it wasn't interesting. Sometimes it was ugly. I needed help with my tubes and drains, and getting to the table or toilet. I needed a dishwasher. I needed my pills, organized practically with my meals. I needed air. There was nothing I found as humiliating as getting help into my shoes, or to empty various bags of waste. That, and being pushed in a heap in my wheelchair through the gardens to the pond, then held up like a marionette and maneuvered amicably through the winding shrubs for an encounter with the grass and the ants.

For a long time, Manuel never complained. He said he was grateful. I went to sleep easily and early, and the hours yawned leisurely for him after the china had been washed and put away. He had free reign over my library, all those old books about photography and painters. Sometimes we looked at them together. I shared everything I knew with him about Latin American silver, African masks, German expressionists.

One night after the moon changed hands with the day, the pain in my shrivelled legs reached a crescendo, and I called out. In the distant edges of my restlessness, I heard a woman's laughter. I heard the clinking of crystal in the far room.

Faithfully, as always, his skinny shadow was beside me before I gave in to the panic of pain. Like a lover, he took my frail hand and pierced me with the morphine I had come to depend on. The sweet relief flooding through me was interrupted with the electricity of my petty jealousy. Of Manuel playing backgammon with a chubby barmaid or cashier, a girl I imagined with curling tendrils and a tangle of charms at her throat.

"I'm here at your beck and call," he said, when eventually he felt the steel blade of my disgust. "I am here for everything you need, without question. But you cannot ask me not to live. I must be able to have visitors since I so seldom get to leave the house. I do not have frequent or rowdy guests, and we make very little noise."

I only nodded and went on pouting. I constantly imagined him writhing underneath her, her given to arching abandon, plump and youthful and able. She was redheaded and round, although I'd never seen her with my own eyes. Her distant voice was low and warm, and whenever I heard it in the house, I would call him with an invented calamity or need.

In retrospect, it was, of course my intention to interrupt them. But that's not how I saw it, there, then, in my confused emotions and desperation. I was not able to bear that life was taking place without me.

Manuel tried to extricate himself and get away a few times, to say he needed to contend with personal matters. He asked for a few days off and then a leave of absence. Each time I rained down on him with a storm of terrible concerns so that he felt too guilty to go. I was a vortex. He began to see me as a ball and chain, instead of as the old artist he cared for and loved, someone who opened his heart and mind and wings to the world.

"Look," Manuel finally said, giving me a formal and final letter of resignation. "I have to go home to Mexico, my father is ill." In the rhythm of the machines that attended to me, I heard a soft tide of ebbing and flowing, followed by a fury of falls, rapids rushing down into an abyss.

I couldn't think of him as a young man with a father or as someone from far away who was homesick. I had made him a lover if only in my mind, and now he was abandoning me. He knew me more intimately than anyone ever had.

"What about her?" I spat viciously through the gummy hose jimmied between my teeth, the thing that brought me air. I felt helpless and naked, as needy as I'd ever been.

"Maria? Yes, yes," he said, "we are both going. Father never stops asking for her, she is the youngest, his favourite."

Raw

after *And Tell Me Today's Not Today*, by Christina Quarles
(USA) contemporary

The air in her lungs is chalk, and her esophagus is a dried-up
river bed. The mouthpiece forcing air in and out of Laine's
lungs on its own schedule has left her parched. The nuclear
donut machine is science fiction, clacking and whirring and
moving robotic, mechanical arms around her. "You won't
see or feel the radiation," the brochure stated emphatically.
"Until later…" Right. The rude ruddy swelling started night
before last. Nipple a raw volcano in the centre of the action.
Her lover's fingers on her, soft, dripping calendula and raw
honey. To mitigate the burns.

In these long moments staring at the back of her eyelids and
at the ceiling while they do their "healing," she has too much
time to think. All she can think about is how dry she is, how
dried up, a shell of her former moist and voluptuous self.
Hell, once, she was absolutely gooey. Huge and round, an
everlasting fountain. Then they pumped her full of poisons,
and she knew before they unplugged her that her ovaries
were over. At her centre, she could feel her walls grinding
like sandpaper against each other, the thinning tissues all
fissure and frazzle now. Any razzle dazzle evaporated like
smoke and mirrors.

Chemical rape, she wrote in her notebook, but crumpled that
page the way they crumpled her body. She threw it away two
days later but that didn't erase the truth of what had been

done. Still, when her partner was palpating her poor diseased titty after, he exclaimed suddenly, *I can't feel it, can you?* And he'd guided her hand to where he was prodding, where the hard, hungry sickness had planted its barnacles. It was crumbling. Smashed now, into tiny angry blasted balls. The remains. By the second infusion, the one that left her for hours on the toilet, praying just to shit someday this week, she couldn't find the pieces at all.

If she made it through all this, she was going to live.

Breathe in, when you're ready, and hold, the disassociated voice came through the equipment. Then, the thing shifting, buzzing, hovering over her like something from Star Trek. She held and held and held.

The pain was terrible, and the steroid puffiness and bald eyelids and scalp made her into a grotesque. Her corpulence turned from goddess abundance into a beached whale in need of a wheelbarrow for mobility. The dead toenails and the mouth sores. Was she even human now? The worst of it, though- she detested more than anything else how selfish this thing made her.

Survival mode: every last thing is now about her. *Me first, me first, me first.* She enjoyed her share of the spotlight, gregarious in nature and good natured. "Vibrant." She'd always loved bright pink lippy and cleavage for days. A larger-than-life personality that she hoped some found endearing. If they didn't, what could she do? It was who she was.

But who was she now? The only one. At the subway elevator, screeching, "Please hold that door for me!" as she tries to speed up, bum leg and cane melding into the low hemoglobin that melted her into molasses. Then again, on the crowded bus upstairs, demanding someone offer her a seat. And at home…she was just grateful that her partner was all in, whether they ended up amputating her breasts or leaving a little something scarred and deformed, but something at least, for him. When was the last time she'd invited him to touch her, or put him against her arid, bleached tongue?

She is finished toasting for today, back tomorrow morning. Every damn day. Rain or shine. The radiotherapist helps her pull the hospital gown together and get her to the dressing room.

"Don't forget to soak the burns in saline," the girl says. Forget? She lives with her boob in a bowl of cool salty water, in front of a fan. But she nods. "Thank you, good night." The compassionate nurse who brought ice cubes for her dry mouth after the surgery looked just as young, but Laine had been shocked and touched when she'd shared that she was also recovering from breast cancer. Halfway to her five-year victory, and just half a year back on the ward. None of it was fair. This girl, that girl, just girls. The darkness there, to have that seed of destruction, that pit of rot, in the very centre of your living, your life. To have that lantern of flesh and blood light taken from you for no damn reason. It made her angrier than Laine knew how to manage. She could not pretend to be that hideous fabrication, the pink-ribbon luchador, all bright and positive and grateful. Those "cancer picked the wrong girl" pajamas and that "bald and beautiful" crap made her cringe. But she could not let the reality of her rage fester too freely inside, or she would be consumed by it. No, she couldn't. Not until this was over.

The Handlers

after *Moses and the Brazen Serpent,* by Peter Paul Rubens
(Belgium, b. Germany) 1609

*"They shall take up serpents; and if they drink any deadly
thing, it shall not hurt them; they shall lay hands on the sick,
and they shall be made well."*
Mark 16:18

She was expecting the sweltering heat of the afternoon and
the wide empty skies, and even the loneliness, the way the
distance between the little towns grew with every winding
turn. But she didn't know how the storybook clouds would
float so close to the windshield, vast fluffy things like spun
sugar mountains just ambling about against the perfect blue.
The very air smelled like candy.

The humidity was wreaking havoc on her joints and her legs
and hands were painfully swollen. Vivian pulled over at a
One Stop for a cold bottle of water and gas and a restroom.
The glossy, generic insides of the sundry store felt
incongruous out here, where miles of ramshackle barns and
other ruins grew covered in vines, and choirs of black-eyed-
susans and bluebells waved across the fields.

"It's them bluebonnets what smell like that," the attendant
told her when she asked about the heady sweet perfume
pervading everything. "Some say it's like fruit punch. We
like to say it's the smell of purple."

Vivian paid and thanked him, surprised when he left his perch behind the counter to get the door for her on the way out. "Take your time, ma'am," he said kindly, "and mind the holes in the asphalt."

In her long sickness, Vivian never got used to the helpfulness of others. She wished she could keep her pain private, but it was written on her body, the way it was already starting to twist up, and in her gait. There were a few years to go before she would be a grandmother, but she already used a cane and there was a walker on standby in the trunk for the occasions that things got worse. She smiled a vague thanks at the young man and went on her way.

The journey so far had been much longer than these twisting miles witnessed by wide-eyed cows and marigolds. Her DNA testing service and private investigator had brought her here, to the hardscrabble lineage of the Scots in Appalachia. Her story was not much different than that of other adoptees: a teenage mother who had simply been too young to keep her baby. The search had been anticlimactic in a sense: her birth mother had died young, ten years or so after giving her up, of breast cancer.

Vivian was still compelled to come to the hills and hollows of West Virginia, whose tiny towns were all but emptied of coal. Each dot on the map held the odd boarded up cluster of houses and shops and a few forgotten folks, chalk-pale people with skinny legs and Pop-Tart bellies. Narrow faces and wary eyes. It was a strange feeling to think that any of them could be a sister or nephew.

Vivian had spent a good part of her desk time the past few months, back in Pittsburgh at the pain clinic where she worked, snooping social media for clues. In her line of work, the phone was always ringing and there was a constant onslaught of emails that needed answering, but she came in early and stayed when the door locked for lunch. But there weren't many Mirror Creek or nearby Dunns on Facebook. The detective she'd hired said plainly that the kind of people she was from didn't have Instagram pages or LinkedIn accounts. Some of them wouldn't even have birth certificates.

Her adoptive family was stable and middle-class and nominally Catholic, giving her a past that was safe and centered. But her origin story was as old as the hills: people who worked their fingers to the bone, had nothing, and lived and died in anonymity.

The only possible relative Dunns she had found had been in the news because of a wacky church that was into snake handling. A fringe minority of Pentecostal Americans were infamous for their bizarre handling rituals, something condemned by mainstream believers. These practices were relegated mostly to the uneducated and the destitute, a legacy of coal mining and isolation.

Vivian had watched a few recordings of their services on Youtube with morbid fascination and disgust. It was just a handful in the congregation, a few men and women clanging on cymbals and spoons and an old washboard, stomping their feet. A few rugged, snaggle-toothed people held up the writhing and venomous things high in their hands, passing them one to another.

It was grainy footage but even so, she found one face compelling. His eyes were beady black holes that glazed over when he took up the serpent and held it high in the air. There was a glow that came over him then. His ecstasy softened his natural features that were as sharp as broken glass. His hands were in motion to the rhythms of their strange gospel, but when she zoomed in, she could see that one middle finger was just a stub. He had been bitten and survived.

She also saw his ears, how the lower part of them was delicate like a shell, almost fused to the tender part of the neck behind them. This caught her attention. David, her husband, had given her the tiniest diamond studs when they were first dating, saying her earlobes were too small for other earrings. She had never bothered with any other earrings.

When all of this had started, David had asked what it was Vivian was looking for. She didn't really have a good answer. Others in her position often said they wanted to know who they really were. But Vivian wasn't so sure how much of one's identity was in the mitochondria and muscle, rather than in experiences and surroundings they shared and the people they shared them with. She loved and was loved by the family she had been placed with, and inside the family she had made. Her parents had never concealed her adoption from her like some families chose to. In fact, she grew up knowing that she had been an answer to prayer. She didn't believe that she was someone else, someone unknown, because of people she had never met. If DNA didn't lie, maybe it wasn't the whole truth, either. Wasn't the body the most transient part of ourselves?

She also understood that few people welcomed finding out they had a relative previously unknown. While such a connection could be meaningful to an individual puzzling together their history, it was irrelevant and intrusive for most on the other side of the story. Learning that a cousin had a secret pregnancy, and half a century later, that offspring wanted to snoop around and get chummy, was more often than not disruptive to people's lives.

Perhaps the simplest answer was pure curiosity. Who wouldn't want to know?

Research and digging was Vivian's way. She had spent years looking for answers that could help explain or manage her battle with inflammatory arthritis. She suspected her doctors, even the specialists, knew nothing about it. They doled out useless pills and smug platitudes. The disease began its assault on her body when she was barely thirty. It was likely she'd be in a wheelchair in another ten years. The treatments and medications they paid thousands for barely slowed its progress. Most scientists and doctors weren't interested in root causes of autoimmune diseases. Almost no progress had been made on the subject in decades, even as the rarest disorders became commonplace.

Vivian had grown tired of this futile research. It wouldn't change anything for her. She started putting her investigative energies into other questions she had. One day she joined an adoptee group online and began searching for answers. She had been learning about Native American medicine and felt an uncanny connection there, feeling quite certain for a while that the clues to her secret history were here. She was surprised to find Scottish roots, assuming they were mostly blue-eyed and red-haired, where she had near black hair and carefully cut cheekbones. As it turned out, the family name itself, Dunn, meant "dark one."

It dawned on her somewhere along the way that she could just go there, to Mirror Creek, where the detective had traced her birth mother. West Virginia was just a few hours away by car from Pittsburgh, not far at all. She booked a few days off from the clinic. And David booked a room for her in a random little town near Mirror Creek, somewhere along the Big Coal River.

"Who knew I married a hillbilly?" David said as he scrolled Expedia for lodging options. His tone was playful, but even so, it rankled down deep in Vivian. Pure luck of the draw, but she was from the most detested lineage on the map. She had in her life made redneck jokes of her own, of course, just like everyone did, but now she felt something protective and defensive growing internally.

The river was beautiful. It meandered at times slowly along, sparkling deep blue under the sky, and grew full and ferocious at various bends. Occasionally Vivian saw bright yellow or red kayaks in the rapids. Ancient shale peered through heavy boscages of ferns. Grand aspens and sycamores and sweet birches swept both sides of the road, and rolling palisades of black pines and loblollies beckoned her deeper into the mountains. Only rarely now did another car pass Vivian's.

The GPS led her to a tiny town in a clearing, nothing more than a few rusty gas pumps and a deserted old schoolhouse. A rickety shack in the gravel parking lot boasted bait and pouches of tobacco. Vivian made her way gingerly over the lot and yanked the door open. The air was swampy inside, and on the dirt-floor were big white buckets of wriggling worms.

When her eyes adjusted from the bright sunlight, she saw a solitary man, around her age, hollow eyes, hollow jaw, sitting and staring straight ahead, unblinking, unperturbed by the flies buzzing around his face. For a moment, she panicked, wondering if he is dead. She startled when he spoke.

"Help you?"

"Oh, sure, thank you very much," Vivian said. "I'm hoping you can help me find my accommodations." She fumbled in her purse for the paper from David. "Here it is. The Finnlaigh." She smiled and handed it to him. "I wasn't expecting a ghost town!"

The man eyed her coldly. "We are not ghosts," he said. "We are real, living people."

Vivian wasn't so sure. The stranger had still not blinked or barely moved. When he handed back the paper, she saw from the gnarled ropes of veins on his fingers that he was much older than she had first suspected.

It was unsettling to wonder whether he could be her kin, and she did not yet have the courage to start asking questions.

But then he directed her a mile up the way, not unkindly. "You're almost there," he said with a tone of reassurance. Vivian looked around under the counter for something she could buy but the earthy smell of worms and the few jars of stale and sticky candies did not appeal. Finally she chose a packet of Halls cough lozenges, for which she had no need.

There were few buildings, just a rundown tire shop and then a pie stand at the side of the road. Vivian backed up the vehicle. A home-baked pawpaw pie or perhaps the legendary local shoofly would make a nice treat later. A dusty tin can had a slot for bills and coins. Vivian picked out a delicious looking peach cobbler, then hesitated, seeing the vinegar pie. In her research, she had learned that the enterprising women of Appalachia had made pie from vinegar when citrus was in short supply. The writer referred to them as "innovation pies."

Vivian decided on both pastries. Then she would have plenty to share. She pushed twice the price asked into the tin, and drove on.

At first she drove right past the Finnlaigh. It wasn't a motel at all, but a residential home. Only the standing mailbox, stuffed full of crumpled, faded flyers, showed the name, in tiny letters. The yard was strewn with hubcaps and blocks of cement. There was a big beech tree, too, with what seemed like hundreds of blue glass bottles tied to its branches, dangling in the breeze and catching the late afternoon light.

It wasn't the first time she'd seen a bottle tree. Further south, they were quite common, a tradition from those Americans stolen from Africa, meant as a way of capturing evil spirits and keeping them out of your house. It took root widely among people who spent many hours on their porches or in their gardens, who saw the custom as quaint and ornamental.

Vivian also knew from her research that the style of dwelling was called a dog-trot house, or deeper into the mountain history, the possum-trot. These homes were built in two sections, sharing a roof, separated with a breezeway at ground level.

This had been the closest room to Mirror Creek that David could find. The snake church was there, but not much else. She'd asked him to look in the vicinity. Not that she was expecting luxury accommodations, but this was someone's house.

In her mind, she had imagined humble lodging with a little tavern downstairs. She could indulge in a few sips of bourbon and get friendly with the locals. There would be some rootsy folk music playing, something curious and ominous, maybe Johnny Cash, maybe Woody Guthrie's "Go Tell Aunt Rhodie." She'd order another, mull over a leftover newspaper, pick the bartender's brain after some liquid courage.

Standing in the sweltering driveway now among sparkling wheels and coloured glass, juggling both pies and her cane, she wished she'd been smarter and booked something generic and private, in Beckley maybe, or Charleston. Driving 30 minutes or more to Mirror Creek wouldn't have been a big deal.

Vivian gathered her guts and rapped on the door. It opened so fast she almost dropped the cobbler. "We've been expecting you!" a booming voice said, and there was a smile just as wide to go with it. The lady of the house, Christine. She was a brassy bottle blonde with a confetti of freckles across her face and arms. "Oh, love, let me take those for you, oh, looks like you got some of Helen's pies, you're going to love these, love." She talked a mile a minute. "Vivian, was it? Heavens, you must be tired. We can make iced tea or a fresh pot of coffee for refreshments. Meanwhile, I'll show you to your room so you can get comfortable."

She led Vivian across the possum runway to the other side's cabin. To Vivian's relief, the room was tidy and homey enough. "Thanks so much, Christine. I was admiring your beautiful bottle tree outside. So lovely." Just to make conversation. Of course she didn't mention the hubcaps.

Something flickered over Christine's face. "Those have a purpose you know," she said. "There are a lot of evil spirits in these parts. Well, they're everywhere, really."

She patted a small stack of towels on a dresser and pointed to a door. "Shower's yonder. You'll feel mighty nice if you cool off before dinner." Christine smiled broadly again. "What brings you out this way? We don't get many visitors."

Vivian looked forward to the cool water and resting her limbs awhile to calm the pain. She studied Christine's face, wondering whether there was a connection. She didn't see any familiar features. She wasn't sure what to say or how to ask, and wondered again whether it had been foolish to make the trip. David's question flashed through her mind. What was she hoping to find?

But she was here now. So she plunged in. "Well, I was hoping to attend church service tomorrow morning, at the House of Holiness, in Mirror Creek."

Another ripple of darkness crossed Christine's sunny face. Her tone grew harsh. "Are you a believer? Or one of those misery tourists from the city, come to mock the country folk?"

Vivian was caught off guard. After a long hesitation, she said, "Neither. Well, I'm a Christian. We are Catholics. Not as devout as we should be."

Christine nodded. "Catholic's better than nothing," she said, and laughed a little to show she meant it lightly. But she waited for Vivian to go on and tell her what her business was there.

It seemed like the best tactic would be to tell it like it was.

"So, I recently learned that my birth mother was a woman named Charlotte Dunn, from Mirror Creek. I understand she died a long time ago. There may be relatives remaining. I hoped to come and find out more about my biological family."

Christine's eyes widened then and softened, too. "Oh, love, that's really something," she said. "Of course I knew Charlotte. Everyone knows everyone around here. So you're the one! Wow! I was still a girl when it all happened. Now, you probably want to rest for a spell but I'll bring your sweets and some drinks and leave them right here on the dresser. We can talk more about this at dinner." She impulsively threw her arms around Vivian and squeezed.

Christine paused then. "Not everyone is friendly with outsiders, here, understand that. People come nosing around with bad intentions. Mountain people have never welcomed interference. We keep to ourselves and ask the same of the world. But also, strangers are often surprised by our kindness. When Charlotte got knocked up, the village supported her. They would have helped her with her child. I remember her saying it broke her apart to lose her baby girl, but that she wanted to make sure you had the best possible circumstances."

Vivian felt the wind being knocked out of her. To hear, so casually, confirmation of her existence, and connection with her mother, felt surreal. She hadn't dared dream that her mother, or any others, had felt love for that baby. Hearing that there was, in some small way, gave her something she couldn't explain, something she didn't know she needed.

Vivian smiled in gratitude. "I'd better sit down," she said.

"I know about the stereotypes out there about the people in these mountains and hollers," Christine continued. "And some of these folks are a little rough around the edges. But personally, for me, I don't believe in shaming Charlotte or anyone else in her situation. The Bible I believe in says the truth will set you free."

Vivian smiled with gratitude. But then Christine said, to her surprise, "How long you been sick, love? Maybe God was calling you home to House of Holiness in more ways than one."

With that she turned and left the room.

Vivian stripped down to her drawers, and put her sore legs up on the bed. That's when she noticed a plaque on the wall, showing a snake made from a mosaic of coloured glass bits. In elaborate calligraphy, it spelled out the verse Vivian knew from her research, Luke 10:19.

"Behold, I give unto you power to tread on serpents and scorpions, and over all the power of the enemy: and nothing shall by any means hurt you."

She slept for a couple of hours. Christine knocked to let her know it would soon be time for dinner. Vivian quickly showered, showing up at the table refreshed. "I didn't want to wake you, so we saved your pies for dessert," Christine said. She introduced her husband, Dale, and he pumped Vivian's hand so vigorously that she winced from the shock of it. "Careful, love," Christine said, tapping him gently on the upper arm. "I told you about her arthritis."

"No worries," Vivian said. "This looks amazing." There was stew and biscuits and green beans and potato salad. "Thank you so much."

When she pronounced the stew delicious, Dale said, "It's got a mess of squirrels in it. I shot them myself." He threw back his head and laughed heartily. Christine slapped him playfully. "Cut that out," she said, reassuring her guest that it was beef.

"What do y'all think we do with all those rattlesnakes?" Dale continued. Vivian chuckled too. The fact that the husband was a bit of a joker took some of the weight out of the air.

"The wife told me that you're Charlotte Dunn's girl," he said later, after Vivian had scarfed down two heaps of "rattler stew" and her weight in potato salad. "I reckon you come full of questions."

Vivian nodded. "Yes. But I understand that most adoptees find out what I have found out already: the reason is almost always a young mother. I have loving parents. I don't need anything. Still, maybe it is only natural that we feel compelled to find out more about our ancestors."

"Did you take one of them gene kit tests?" Dale asked.

"Oh, yes. I am mostly Scottish, with flecks of Irish, English, and German. The test didn't name any specific relatives. They explained that said relatives would have to have registered themselves. My paperwork told me the name and place of my birth mother."

Vivian paused. "I am not expecting any grand reunions. I just hoped to spend a few days here to experience the place I came from. I don't have any information on paternity- I don't know who my father was."

Dale laughed loudly again, actually slapping his legs with both hands. "Everyone around here knows your Daddy was the Skelton boy. Matthew. Charlotte was head over heels in love with him."

The whole matter felt, again, anticlimactic and strange. So Vivian was an open secret. Of course, the Finnlaighs could be mistaken. But they weren't the type to make something up.

Dale grew more serious then. "She wouldn't marry him, though. He was already by then hard into the booze, just like his daddy had been. He's long passed now, too. His liver got him young."

So they were both gone, then. Vivian felt a pang of grief.

Even so, it was already much more than she was expecting to know.

"The wife tells me you might be interested in handling, too," Dale said next, then started laughing again.

"Well, no. I do want to attend the service in the morning, but I'll worship in my own way and watch and learn from the others."

"We can all go together," Christine said. "That way, it will be easier for you to meet the community."

It was that weird feeling again, unfamiliar and intangible, the emotions there, that she would be among relatives. She was grateful for the Finnlaighs' offer, to buffer that transition.

"I understand that there are just a few...Holiness churches...left," Vivian said. "And the tradition was born right here in these mountains and valleys in the early 1900s?"

"So they say," Christine said.

"Oh, no, it's much older than that," Dale said. He gestured to a painting in the other room, then got up to turn on the lights and beckon Vivian over for a closer look.

The print was of a 17th century artwork, depicting a Biblical scene. There was a viper wrapped around a pillar and a prostrate crowd before it. "This is something that took place 5000 years ago," Dale told her. "Do you know the story of the snakes in the wilderness? God sent thousands of snakes because he was angry at the Israelites for their idolatry and blasphemy. Many of them were bitten. God then told Moses to make a bronze snake on a tree. Anyone who saw it would be healed from the venom by the Lord. God was mocking the concept of an idol, reminding them that He had all the power. And the tree foreshadowed the crucifixion."

Vivian hadn't thought much about these old Sunday School stories in years. Of course she recalled the snake as the Devil's face in the story of the fall of man. Yet, as the story went, God ultimately had the power over evil and death.

"You must be familiar with John 3," Dale said. Vivian nodded.

"Of course. The most famous verse of all. 'For God so loved the world…'"

"And the verse before it?"

She shook her head, ashamed. "I don't recall."

"And just as Moses lifted up the serpent in the wilderness, so must the Son of Man be lifted up," Dale recited from heart.

"Handling is not for everyone," Christine said. "But it's not something crazy, either. It's the oldest story in the book. If we believe Christ is the Great Physician, then we shall fear no evil. And the snake was the God-given symbol of evil from the beginning."

"We welcome death," Dale went on. "If God wills it. It's not about being reckless. It's about accepting the absolute reality of the inevitable, in full trust that there is more here than our bodies. Everything you see anywhere in the world, it's about people trying to cheat death. And it simply can't be done. We have chosen to accept that the author of life and death is not under our control or command. If that author extends our life, so be it. If He heals us, the glory belongs to Him. No sense in trying to outrun the truth about death. No one can. No one ever has. It's really very simple."

That night, Vivian dreamed about Eve, and Eden, and all the caverns of coal underneath these hills, those deserted and those still blooming alike. In her dream, these pits were hell, black and molten, and the mines were filled with snakes.

She dreamed of a young couple, the young girl with raven tresses just like hers had been. The lovers couldn't keep their hands off of each other, and in their frenzy, she watched herself forming from the dust of the coal mines. The same dust God had made into Adam in the mists of time.

In the morning, her ankles were burning badly and her loosest sneakers barely fit. Vivian popped a few pills and downed a hearty breakfast from her generous hosts. Then, she stepped with them over the threshold of the House of Holiness.

The church wasn't much to look at. It had been converted from an old garage. Four concrete walls, a concrete floor, small windows. A simple cross made out of beams at the front. There was a heap of discarded crutches and other medical paraphernalia underneath it. There were glass and wooden boxes, large as old ocean trunks, of wriggly copperheads and other venomous snakes. There were more vipers than congregants, who numbered barely two dozen.

Vivian knew without a doubt that some of them were her relatives. But now there was another feeling, the sense that their bond ran still deeper than genes and chromosomes.

When the sermon finished, some of the faithful picked up a tambourine or a banjo. They started to sway and stomp their feet. The mountain versions of the old hymns seemed somehow familiar to Vivian. She felt them deep down. She watched with fascination as the serpents were taken out of the boxes, and the handlers passed them around.

With their hands in the air, these people, her people, Vivian felt God in the midst. *For He is high and lifted up…*

She made eye contact with the one with the small earlobes. There was a jolt of recognition, as if she was staring through time. The man was bathed in that same fever she had seen before, confident as he handled the mysterious creature, wrapped it around his shoulders.

No words were exchanged, but as if Vivian was somewhere else, or someone else, she saw her cane fall and her hands reaching up to take the snake. And then she surrendered, falling, or flying, into the place beyond the pain.

The End

after *Untitled (Say Goodbye, Catullus, to the Shores of Asia Minor)* by Cy Twombly (USA) 1994

Thin sliver of crepuscule, ghost light slit, comes under the hospital blinds like a dirty fingernail. You as faint as paper, mottled bruises bleeding underneath your eyes, up and down your arms like asters, like dark roses.

You still breathing heavy. The stink of it. I would have skipped all this if I could.

You wag a crooked finger at the window. Said you heard an always knocking. Your Mutti and Vati, everyone you knew, on the other side of that window.

You are crossing now, I tell you, and everything unsaid between us is an open wound.

Donkey Milk

after *Cosmos All Day Breakfast Diner,* by Carole Spandau (USA) contemporary

Dennis is already waiting for her in the car when she sees the new blisters in the under-moon of her breast. Daphne was still towelling off when she heard his keys jingle as he slipped out the door. He is always eager and early, even on relaxed Sunday mornings.

She imagines him sitting there patiently behind the wheel, fiddling with the radio dial. He doesn't mind waiting for her, but still she wishes she could keep up with him.

Right now she's focused on the sprinkling of raw welts cropping up under the flaccid remains of a once glorious tit. It's itchy, and when she runs her fingers there it is quite painful.

Ugh, what now? It was so humid yesterday. She rummages through the bathroom apothecary for steroid cream. She finds a jar of Boswellia oil from Barbara for some other skin problem. Daphne slathers it over the rash, then covers it with a square of gauze. She doesn't tape it down- she still has bright red marks across her chest from the heart scan, adhesive burns from the electrodes. The bandage will stay in place okay with her bra.

Daphne has always had sensitive skin. But she thinks a lot of this is the toxic side effects of all those horse pills she pops: thyroid meds, hormone blockers, blood pressure pills, antihistamines, diuretics…

"Anyhow, here in one piece," she says, landing in place in the passenger seat. Dennis is whistling to The Eagles and lightly drumming the steering wheel in time to the beat. "*I want to sleep with you in the desert night…with a billion stars all around…*" They did do that, once, when they were young and free, made love in the back of his pick-up truck under an ocean of stars not far from the Grand Canyon.

Daphne knows Dennis is thinking about it too- it's why he loves this old song whenever it comes on.

They sing along, pulling into their usual spot at the Fresh and Friendly just as the last refrain fades away. Dennis squeezes her arm gently while he helps unbuckle her. "All good?" he asks. "Good enough," she replies.

Will and Barbara are already inside, holding their table. Will and Dennis used to play baseball together, going way back to high school. But all of them are just getting to know Barbara. It was always Will and Margo, until they lost Margo to pancreatic cancer five years past. Margo, Daphne's lifelong best friend.

Barbara is lovely, loud and warm and funny. She has a Florida tan despite the New England winters, although rather more chalky and peach-toned. Barbara likes to show off her enviable legs in cowgirl boots and tight stretchy jeans. Up top, she's got nothing left to flaunt after three runs with breast cancer, with "both girls amputated to the pavement," in her own words.

The waitress comes, a shy and plump thing with rings in her nose and lips. "Oh, that one's just darling," Barbara wheezes in her smiley sing-song voice, tapping the centre groove above her lip. She orders more coffee and fresh-squeezed lime juice, no sugar, and three eggs over easy with organic farmer's sausage and a side of greens.

Barbara has been extolling the virtues of keto but Daphne has been ordered to eat low fat and low sodium. She orders dry sourdough toast and an egg white mixed veggie omelette. Both of the men order a stack of pancakes with syrup and a peameal bacon sandwich. "It's all organic here," Will likes to say, which is enough to take the worry out of it for those two. Every week, Barbara and Daphne look wistfully at their men's greasy, carb-laden platters while they make do with their own choices.

After brunch, the four usually head to the farmer's market. Barbara likes to get pastured meats from some of the Amish sellers. Daphne gets bundles of chard and fresh herbs. They both love to amble through the craft stalls, too. While Daphne confides her latest rash woes, Barbara picks out some beeswax tea lights. "Oh, you know, you should put honey on those rashes," she says, excitedly wrapping her manicured fingers around a jar of local wildflower honey. "Always raw," she says, tapping the label where it says "unpasteurized." It was probably true: Daphne remembered how her grandmother had put honey on their skinned knees when they were wee, and how those scrapes dissolved like magic. She holds the jar up to catch the clerk's eye.

"And donkey milk soaps, too," Barbara is saying. "Donkey milk is anti-fungal and anti-inflammatory. It's full of magical fatty acids and enzymes!" Barbara is always reading posh glossy magazines full of ancient health and beauty secrets. "Not too many sellers out there, probably have to order it online, but we'll find some," she promises. "The company I read about orders from donkeys in the Azores. Oh, I just know it will soothe your flare ups nicely."

Daphne misses her friend Margo all the time. Margo was quieter and her beauty was more subtle. She wore rubber Wellington boots and left her hair gray, and she could probably milk the damn donkeys herself. Will had been just broken to lose her. Daphne too still cries some days for Margo, remembering how gaunt and empty she'd been near the end.

But Barbara is special, too. She never dismisses or minimizes Daphne's aches and pains, and she listens so carefully. She's nurturing with all of her creams and lotions. Daphne imagines how she must have nursed Will back to life when he was dead inside, made him feel something again. She imagines when he cuts himself shaving, how Barbara might dip her soft peach fingertip into acacia honey, run her sweetness along his wounds. She sometimes wonders what will become of Dennis when she's gone. She hopes he'll let himself find someone like her friend.

Thursday

after St. Elizabeth of Hungary Bringing Food for the Inmates of a Hospital, by Adam Elsheimer (England) 1598

It's the fourth time she has called Mother today, but the nurses or aides never answer the phone. Unacceptable.

Megan fumes, but she knows the place is perpetually understaffed. The few people who are willing to work there are overworked and exhausted. She has to be grateful someone is there at all.

When Megan finally gets through, the weight of her mother's loneliness is almost too much to bear. It takes Mary a long time to pull a sentence out. Megan can practice patience and wait for her words, but there aren't many who are willing at the home. The other inmates don't bother. They are hard of hearing, or in pain, or just not interested. It is a terrible irony that Mary is surrounded by dozens of others, but can talk with no one. Her disease has also affected her vision, so she can't read her romance novels anymore, either. She just sits there, waiting to die and wishing she would.

Mary asks Megan the same thing she always asks. Can she come home and live with her? Megan sees no point in beating around the bush and giving Mother false hope. She explains every time that it is impossible. She is hardly there, between work and all of her own medical appointments and therapies. And Mary needs care around the clock.

Megan's oldest brother gets impatient with the repeated requests, says Mother is trying to wangle her agenda. He can't help her either. His house is not equipped for a wheelchair. And he has two teenagers on his hands, one who is on the spectrum and non-verbal, the other with a serious drug problem.

Mother finally spits out her sentence, which Megan knows was meant to be snapped short and bitterly. "I have two kids and none of them want me." She goes on to ask if Megan convinced Brian not to take her in, or vice versa.

It isn't ideal, but Megan can only get out there to see Mother every other month. She simply cannot take time off to leave town, even though it's just a few hours away. She has been at the edge of bankruptcy for years, thanks to her own battles, lupus, a horrible disease. After she got Covid she could hardly get out of bed for a year and couldn't stop coughing for months. With so many appointments, she has to work weekends and evenings, and she still can't make ends meet.

It may be true that Brian resents Mary's manipulations, and that Megan barely ever comes to see her, but it's not true that they don't care. Brian shoulders responsibilities and anxieties that Mother couldn't begin to understand. He had to learn how to be a loving father to a son with severe challenges. He's sure the neglect of the other son contributed to his wayward path.

For Megan, fighting to stay afloat and stay alive, she still carries a terrible guilt around like a dead weight. It's hell to be a prisoner of your own body, something she understands first-hand.

Megan tells Mother that she will pray for her comfort and peace each day. It is better to empathize with her suffering and humiliation, to acknowledge it. She is helpless herself to help, but she knows all too well how real that pain is.

It's also true that Mother never did and won't now start considering the needs and struggles of her children. Instead of comforting her son or saying she is proud of him, she just barks that the grandkids never visit. She never wanted much to do with them when she was free, however. Mary often said a good spanking was all Kyle needed to make him start talking.

Megan sometimes wonders about the order of things, about the way things happen. People always said that everything happens for a reason: they believed that there must be some kind of cause and effect. Megan's experiences and observations don't match this certainty held by others. She would go so far as to think it's just a commonly held delusion, a belief that keeps people from going totally bonkers.

The way she sees it, it's really more of a lottery. Karma is random, not judicial or moral. You get what you get.

It can't happen now, in any event, what Megan wants most. Closure, reconciliation, understanding. If Mary had never been able to see her offspring as humans with desires and challenges of their own, she wasn't going to start now. But

Megan couldn't just shrug away the burden she carried for Mother's isolation and slow demise... because she wasn't like her. So she lives with the guilt.

Anyways. She's running late. Megan works reception at the hair salon tonight, one of several jobs she's juggling. She opens a cupboard, downs a few pills and a handful of vitamins with a quick cup of yogurt and banana. She grabs a boiled egg. She can eat it on the bus.

Crushed between a bunch of young women heading to the cinema, she pulls out her daytimer, triple checking there isn't anything urgent she's forgetting about. *Call Mother,* it says in today's calendar slot, right before, *salon, 5 to 10.* She crosses it off today's to-do list, moves it as well to Sunday's.

The Nightjar

after *Saint Agatha,* by Carlo Dulci (Italy) 1600s

for Jane Kristen Marczewski

"You can't wait until life isn't hard anymore, before you decide to be happy." Nightbirde

It's not okay, it's not, no, no, how a young girl's gifts fall to shatter. You are as fragile and shy as you pretend you're not: the cancer has taken you down to bare bones. Your courage is a clear bell, and your song in the night is a knife to the spine. You will not make it through this darkness. No golden buzzer will save you. But your sweet voice, the sound of your dreams, might save us.

The Voyeur

after the art of Mari Katayama

From a distance, she is a mermaid, washed ashore, tangled in seaweed and draped across the white sand. The sun rise is gold fire dazzling the horizon and he can't make out the details that would dispel the illusion. So he moves closer. Still can't make sense of the scene in front of him. A spellbinding young woman's torso is blooming from a heap of forms like wriggling tentacles. Closer still, he sees she is seated on a throne of plush satin snakes, crudely stitched and bedazzled in sequins and jewels and lace. She is wearing a kind of corset, cream coloured with trailing ribbons. For a long time he stands concealed in the shadows of a black pine and watches her moving her hands rhythmically. The silhouette of one hand looks like the beak of a gray heron and he wonders if her hands are speaking with some kind of signs. But after observing a while more, he realizes the flicker of copper fireflies are shiny beads and that she is sewing. Eventually, he thinks to take out his phone and make use of the camera zoom. The woman puts her sewing down, endless ropes of cream and rose gold pearls, wrapped around and around the silk and canvas cushions she is seated on. He sees that they resemble something like her own limbs, one of which reaches just under her knee and tapers sharply like a spear, the other rounding closed above where her knee would be. The unexpected beauty of her in her corset with her damaged legs startles him and he feels a strange ripple of attraction. Now she is turning her face to the sky slowly, arching her back like a swan or a dancer, wriggling and flipping to and fro among the gem-crusted cushions, with the gentle jewelled gold waves of water rippling behind her. After watching awhile longer, he sees there is a tripod stationed in the sand. She is taking pictures of herself. He puts his phone back in his pocket and just watches the beach and the beautiful girl and the graceful movement of the black pines along the coast. The girl has become as still as a statue and stays frozen. It takes some time before he realizes that she is also holding a small camera in her bird hand, that she is watching him.

Sick Bed Blues

after *Delta Blues,* by Em Kotoul (USA, b. Czech Republic)
contemporary

for Nehemiah Curtis "Skip" James (1902-1969)

Nehemiah had long disappeared, slipping into the southbound currents of the Mississippi river, and his music with him. Missing, assumed murdered, they all said. It was three decades since he'd sold his guitar. And if his fingers itched at first to pluck and rap that smooth curved body like a drum, well, the way he used to tell it was that he cut them plain away and carried on the work that needed doing.

After awhile, they forgot who he was, and maybe it was just as well. He forgot it, too. The manic frenzy that could overtake him at the juke joint piano, the strange ghostly presence that came up through him when he picked those strings in that intimate way he did.

They said he was the only bluesman in the delta who was a genius on both piano and guitar. No one taught him to play: he'd just learned it himself, from listening as carefully as he could, then working out his songs in his own way. Even so, it was his voice that stood out, high and mournful, as beautiful as a woman's. The cussing clatter and stomp of the gambling crowds always fell to a hush when it was his turn. Flying chairs and breaking bottles froze mid-air until his songs were done. Someone said he sounded otherworldly, like a ghost, or a rare bird keening from the dark bayou.

Nehemiah knew deep down anyhow that his gifts belonged to the devil. A conjure man had told him as much and urged him to outrun his hexes. There was a player from Greenwood that Nehemiah taught for awhile, young Robbie Johnson. Kid stole Neemie's songs and sold them to the rich people who came to hear him play. There was all kinds of talk of a crossroads curse, and whatever it was, Robert was dead before he turned 28. Nehemiah wasn't going out like that.

Before the blues, and then again after, Neemie had gone riding the rails with his Bible and his gun, preaching repentance and dodging bullets, just like his Daddy before him had done. The man he'd never known. Nehemiah had the kind of face you couldn't read and that came in handy for cleaning up when playing cards, but sweeping those little towns clean of their spare coins while preaching hellfire never made him any friends. Everyone liked him better when he made strong mountain dew and passed it around good and cheap, and that paid a hell of a lot better than any piano bar.

The best he'd ever done for money was arranging dates between hungry men and willing women, and standing cross-armed nearby to protect the girls if anyone got unruly. Neem could clean up on corn whiskey, women, and card tables on the weekend, and shiny himself up for Sunday morning, taking any offers for lunch that came his way. After thanking his hosts for the plates of oysters, macaroni, and strawberry Jello, he slipped away, following whatever small town was calling him next.

But all that money was gone now, and blues or no blues, he'd been cursed the whole way through. He was as wretched as he'd ever been, stuck in a sweltering hole in the back of a godforsaken hospital, some nowhere town of 500. He was a eunuch now. The doctors had amputated everything that made him a man. That once proud rooster had been covered in festering tumours. Nehemiah knew the cancer was bad hoodoo juju, and probably from the latest of his ex-wives. Ladies had their ways of keeping a man on a leash.

Neemie thinks he's dead and gone to glory when he stirs from a few days of slumber to find a choir of round white faces staring down at him. He smiles, surprised and pleased to find himself with the angels after all. But it's something else.

"Skip James!" They're saying his old name, over and over. In the heat and in the muddle of his mind and the throes of stabbing pain at his severed centre, it's hard to make sense of all that they're saying. Turns out these three white kids have been hunting him down, hoping he'll be their surprise star for an upcoming music festival.

The first words he's spoken in days: "Son, I haven't played a guitar for thirty years." Neem rings the nurse's bell so that she'll fill him back up with morphine. The hollow fire in his pit is as much pain as he's ever known. Then one of the kids says he's going out to his car. He returns with a guitar, one Nehemiah can barely recognize. For a moment, he misses his Stella, and the stab is near as bad as the hole between his legs.

"Pass it to me," Neemie commands the kids. He starts teasing the strings, and writes a song right there, on the spot.

"I'm layin' sick, honey, and on my bed…I'm laying sick, honey, and on my bed…I used to have some friends, but they sure wish I was dead…in awful pain and deep in misery…"

That strange magic comes up from Nehemiah's bones like a man raised from the dead. Just like that, a song is born, and by nightfall, two more. A few more dozen are burning through from his insides and will soon come to light.

Oh, sure, the white kids will parade him about at the folk revival. They'll keep all his money and his recordings. He'll still die from the cancer his old lady cursed on him: he has only three years left. But Nehemiah doesn't care. He is plugged in again. He is pulling the music from heaven and hell and it's coming through him. He remembers who he is.

Cuckoo

after *Black Forest Music Cuckoo Clock,* by Albert Schwab
(Germany) contemporary

After Maggie's cholecystectomy, the nurse handed George
instructions for adopting a "low-fat, plant-based diet" and
sent them on their merry way. George dutifully pinned it to
the refrigerator door.

He was surprised a few days later to find that the printout
had been scrawled over with crayons, including what looked
to him like a devil, complete with a pitchfork and little horns
on its head.

It was true that the suggested supplies of whole grains, leafy
green veggies, and tofurkey were the same ones he'd been
slugging home in those reusable bags for years. A decade
ago, when the diagnosis of the day was breast cancer, they
had both given up cream and endured their morning coffees
with those chalky, stringy clumps of soy milk that people
pretended to like. They hadn't been big meat eaters at all, but
banished permanently from their table anything red or
marbled or still wearing its skin. There wasn't much on the
recommendation sheet that they hadn't already been using.
But perhaps they could add purslane and millet to their
shopping list.

"Did you draw over this gallbladder care handout?" George
asked Maggie when she shuffled into the kitchen for water.

Maggie laughed. "Who else?" She looked around. "It's just us here. Guilty as charged."

George was glad to see she was feeling better. She'd been through worse, he supposed. A lot of people they knew had had their gallbladders removed.

"Was there something on this list you don't care for?" he asked. "No point picking up stuff we won't use."

Maggie surprised him by reaching over and pulling the paper from the fridge, crumpling it with one hand and tossing it at the compost bin. "Basket," she said.

It was a week or so after that when George returned from some errands and found a massive box on the welcome mat, addressed to Maggie. He dragged it inside. "Special delivery!" he called. He could smell something garlicky and delicious and there was a pleasant sizzling sound that he had not heard in years. "Pork chops?" he asked. He couldn't believe it.

Maggie grinned at him. As if it was nothing out of the ordinary, she said, "I got this luscious recipe from my sister. She posted it on Facebook." He noticed that Maggie was wearing an electric wallop of purple lipstick, and there was an open bottle of something on the go. It looked like Champagne.

While something gooey and peppery bubbled away, Maggie attacked the side of the big box with a pair of scissors. "All the way from Germany!" she exclaimed, wrestling a large wooden from layers of bubble wrap. It was a giant cuckoo clock. George recalled how one year, early in their marriage, at a German Christmas market, Maggie had admired the quirky clocks. He wanted to indulge her, but she declined his offer, saying that their money should be more sensibly spent.

"Wow!" he said, at a loss for words. But he was pleased about it. Maggie had always wanted one. Her grandparents were from the Black Forest mountains where cuckoo clocks were made.

He was more worried about the bubbly. It was not likely recommended to consume alcohol so soon after the surgery. Maggie seldom bothered with the stuff, even at weddings or their trip to Cuba, when everyone else was living it up.

"Everything okay, love?" he asked.

"No," Maggie replied abruptly. "Not really. I'm pretty sure there's another tumour growing…in my other breast." She fumbled with the stovetop dial, moved the meat off the heat. Then, "Do you mind getting plates for us?"

George felt a stabbing inside him, shock and fear. He wasn't sure he could watch her go through more. There had been so much pain, so many pills and procedures. It seemed like they spent half their lives at various clinics and hospitals, with her getting poked and prodded and scanned and cut open and pumped full of medicines.

She never complained, but it didn't seem fair when her peers were growing their careers or getting ready for grandchildren.

He got out the plates, and pulled down another glass while he was at it. Poured it half full. What the hell.

"Are you sure?" he asked, finally.

"No," Maggie said. "I'm not sure. But I'll be surprised if it's something else. Everything feels exactly the same as it was."

George watched in amazement as Maggie downed two chops. When he was done his, he asked her where she wanted to put the clock. The unexpected cuckoo certainly made the room more colourful. "Look," he assured her when he was finished the installation. "If it's bad news, we will just keep doing everything that needs doing, just like always."

Maggie laughed. "I'm done," she said. "I can't do any of that anymore. I'm sorry.'

She pulled a decorative carton from the fridge. "I ordered dessert," she told him. She put a few beautiful little pastries out before him. They were pale green and exquisite, with a citrusy perfume. "They're lime cheesecake bites," she explained.

"Delicious," George said. It was true. And really, what more was there to say? Maggie seldom indulged in sweets or treats, usually quite obsessed with avoiding toxins and junk like sugar. He had never seen her lick cream cheese icing from her fingers and reach for seconds, then thirds.

"We're having red meat again tomorrow night," Maggie told him. "And no salad."

"I suppose that's okay," George replied. "I know you're going through a lot right now. But I'm just a bit concerned that things are getting a little impulsive!"

"Maybe," Maggie said, reaching for the bubbly to refill her glass, then taking a long swig straight from the bottle. "But I no longer give a damn."

Gymnastics

after *Knee Joint,* by Beth Eckel (USA) contemporary

And after a half-dozen aborted attempts to align themselves carnally, they both dissolve in gales of laughter. The technicalities, synovial, fascial, and related to the meniscus. His crooked member and her thighs as broad and bumpy as baked Idaho yellows. Doing it at sixty is nothing like the movies.

Gavage

after *Fat Betty on a Chair,* by Ducian Kay (USA) contemporary

Everyone knew about the fat woman on the fourth floor. Few of us had ever seen her, but we knew she was there.

Every tenant had been in the elevator with a delivery guy, toppling under a tower of pizzas or bag after bag of moo shu pork and fried rice. We knew he was headed to suite 409.

And we saw her husband coming from his car with multiple supersize packs of Lucky Charms and Oreos and Pepsi.

I'd been in the building for a decade and had only laid eyes on her a handful of times. Roberta seldom went anywhere, but once or twice a year there was a sighting. They were painful occasions to witness. The walker she needed could barely support her frame. She shuffled and heaved, inching laboriously along the corridor, in real danger of toppling over. Henry was the skinny sort, wiry and small. She was a giantess, with rolls upon rolls, and hanging fat lobules. It was tragic and grotesque, something best hidden behind closed doors.

Of course, most of the residents were busy with their manufacturing or custodial jobs, their commutes and their families, and we didn't think about Roberta and Henry often. There was laundromat gossip among tenants, smart remarks about the recycling bins overflowing with take-out refuse. There were muffled sympathies for Henry.

I had myself felt quite sorry for Henry for many years, imagining the stigma he bravely shouldered while enduring his wife's gluttony. But one day I ran into him in the convenience store, and something about the demanding way he spoke to the young clerk changed my mind. He berated her for something inconsequential like she was the help, and his controlling tone took me by surprise. I did my best after that to steer clear of Henry.

It was on a weekend that Roberta fell in the parking lot, trying to get to a van taxi. There was no sign of Henry, just her and the walker that teetered and veered dangerously under her meaty paws. Everyone saw her then: it was sunny and folks were walking their dogs or kicking a ball around the grass with the kids, and the laundromat was always busy on Saturdays. We watched, compelled by the accident that could so easily happen, as she heaved herself toward the van. No one, not even the beefy construction workers, would be able to help her up.

And then the accident happened. Roberta fell.

It was terrible to watch, an excruciating, slow-motion film. The heft of her, pushing forward, with just a few more metres to the vehicle. She slipped, and the walker moved away from her, and her ankle turned, and there was a terrible cracking sound, and then there was a deep, guttural wail, like all the air being let out of balloon, or a life. And she went down, the mountain of her, rolling and rolling down onto the tarmac like an avalanche.

We all froze for several moments, and then everyone rushed over all at once. The cab driver got out. We all looked down at the woman we lived beside and never spoke to. The pinhole eyes behind her swollen face stared out at us unblinking. Her mouth was greasy as it opened and closed soundlessly, and something about that made me sadder than I'd ever been.

It took another few moments of confusion and commotion to figure out that we would need to call someone. One lady leaned over and asked if Henry could come out to help her. Roberta's walrus-body shook some then, and a sound like a belch rang from her. The mechanic with his beagle eventually tapped 911 into his mobile. Mrs. Xi was on her way to find Henry, but decided to fetch some water for Roberta instead, so I was appointed to go up. Oola, the big and colourful lady from West Africa lived on the fourth floor, so she came along, too. In the elevator, adjusting her many scarves, she told me something that chilled me to the core. "That girl is a victim of leblouh, like I was," she said.

I had no idea what she meant, but by the time we knocked on Henry's door and found no one there, and returned to the parking lot empty-handed, I learned how young girls from Nigeria and Mauritania were chained down for months and force-fed mountains of grains and animal fat by their mothers, fattening them up for marriage.

She explained that it was an old custom, still practiced in remote rural regions, and compared it to the way geese are force-fed in factories for the French supposed-delicacy of foie-gras. *Gavage.*

Roberta was probably born and raised right here in Scarborough. But just as I started to protest Oola's declaration, I recalled skimming a tabloid article about a girl whose boyfriend wanted her to eat obscene amounts of food. The couple called it "erotic feeding." The boyfriend said it was a humiliation and submission thing. He wanted her to get so fat she couldn't move and had to depend on him completely. I was disgusted with the story and turned the page. I never thought about it again, until now.

The paramedics were working with Roberta when we returned and the tenants were all gathered to one side of the lot. Oola asked me how they would get her into the ambulance, and I said they were probably trained to hoist a pulley of some kind. But it turned out to be too late anyways. I couldn't stay outside to gawk then, it just wasn't right, and there was nothing more I could do to help, so I went inside.

Henry didn't turn up until later. Mr. Xi drove him to the morgue.

It turned out Roberta had had a massive stroke.

I couldn't shake the feeling that she had been trying to get away.

The Minotaur

after *Science and Charity,* by Pablo Picasso (Spain) 1897

The painter's clients and acquaintances might be surprised, and especially his lovers, how tender he had been as a child. The earliest photographs reveal a small boy with an impish spirit already showing in his eyes. There is confidence and determination, too. Some children are born already knowing who they are and what they want, and he was one of them. He knew by the time he could talk that he would be a greater painter than even his father.

But there is a softness there, too, and it makes him almost pretty. You can see it even more in the face of his younger sister, who is the spitting image of him in feminine form. But the boy's innocence was irreversibly shattered on that precarious ledge between child and adult. Going to mass was the tradition for every Spanish family on Sundays. At thirteen, his father took him afterwards to another kind of church, where he was initiated into the pleasures of the flesh by women twice his age. That same season, the young man watched his beloved little sister suffer the agonies of Christ, coughing for months as she grew thinner. Doctors came and went from her little room, but they could not save her. The boy was inconsolable when they took her tiny body away forever.

That was twenty years ago, but he relives his helplessness and fury all over again with Eva. The first woman that he truly loved refused to marry him. She understood him too well, perhaps, and knew that his art would be his only wife. He loves Eva even more, and though she loves him, too, she, too, refused the vows she knew he could not keep. Like a cruel replay of the past, she coughed through their happiest years together. Not diphtheria, but cancer of the throat. Her bloody handkerchiefs littered his room alongside his turpentine rags and hundreds of canvases.

The painter shares his pain with his good friend Gertrude in a letter. Life has been hell, he writes, in and out of hospitals. And then, after: "My poor Eva is dead. This has been a great sorrow. She was so good to me."

In his loneliness there, in those brief moments between Eva and his next conquest, he thinks about the secret pact he had made so long ago with the authorities in the heavens. If only his beautiful sister would live, he would lay down his brushes for her and give up his glory. There was nothing he loved more than painting. Creativity was his divine gift. It moved inside of him like thunder, like a raging river. But he would give it all up if the Lord would renew her to life.

His sacrifice was inadequate, or perhaps it fell on deaf ears. Bargaining for mercy with his very soul had been futile. Now, as then, he understands. There is no benevolent force, no personal love, no mercy, in the mystery of fate. It is every man for himself. All right then. He would be the omnipotent one, the creator and destroyer, the greatest artist who ever lived. I, King, he had once signed a painting. In that moment, he had vowed to become the greatest artist who ever lived. Picasso, as epic and brutal as God.

Dancing Queen

after *Exotic Dancers*, by Gaston Bussiere (France) 1880

For years they had enjoyed walking together every evening. Some fresh air felt nice after dinner, and they never grew tired of happy dogs flinging themselves from one end of the park to the other. Carrie's legs were so bad now that just walking to the end of the block and back was an ordeal, but more often than not, they still went, going slowly with her walker and enjoying the falling sun or early stars.

Gary liked to look inside the houses as they passed and imagine what the people were doing, what they'd had for dinner, what kind of TV programs they liked best. Carrie liked to take her shoes off and put her feet right down on the grass if they made it as far as the park. Gary couldn't do that. He couldn't even wear sandals. She didn't care about germs or dog pee. She said she could feel the whole earth inside of her aching bones.

Tonight they stop at Choi's because it's open late and Gary feels like a bit of chocolate. He surprises Carrie with a lime popsicle.

"I don't want to be without you, ever," he says.

"No chance of that," she replies, catching the dayglow green drips from her ice treat. "There's no one else left on my dance card. I threw my little black book away a long time ago." She laughs.

"That's not what I mean," he says. Of course she knows that.

"Don't worry. You're going to die before me. And then what will I do?"

They both giggle. But they've actually talked about the possibility of some kind of pact. Neither wants to be left behind when the inevitable comes.

He'd been married and divorced three times and owned next to nothing thanks to all that alimony. She didn't care about his past mistakes in life and love. She had her own to contend with. Carrie had never been married before. She had worked for years as a dancer, and then at a truck stop selling cigarettes. She didn't have anything either. And she didn't want anything. When they met, she said she didn't know many men who would forgive a woman for showing off her beauty while she had it.

Even though Carrie's years of erotic escapades far outnumbered his, he wasn't counting. He didn't understand men who were jealous about a woman who lived in her body and enjoyed it while she could. Or who did what she had to. And he understood too, that sometimes those were the same thing.

They couldn't have known they'd still spend a quarter century together. And still, more years left to go. They still took care of each other in all the ways they could. She let him suckle at her nipples when he couldn't sleep, even when his teeth were in a glass of Polident in the bathroom. Her breasts were soft and slack but he loved them. She still enjoyed running her fingers across him and he thought her hands were especially elegant. He still loved to give her pleasure and wore the oud cologne that used to have her climbing the walls, hands greedy all over him.

Sometimes when she was snoring softly he would finish things off for himself. Usually he didn't need to or couldn't muster the destination. This part of himself these days was more about being close, or sharing a moment together. But sometimes that was there, even now, staring eighty in the balls. In those moments, he imagines her dancing, spinning sweaty to Def Leppard or Journey. The joint smelling like Dentyne and pickles and cheap perfume.

Her old work a lifetime ago was something she would only bring up jokingly. She was sad, she admitted once, that once she had belonged to everyone but him.

But Gary didn't see it that way at all. From here he still pictured her as he knew she really was, beautiful, wild, and free.

Storm Chasers

after *Untitled (Storm Over the Haunted Castle),* by Zdzislaw
Beksinski (Poland) before 2005

Dreaming fire again. Distant drum of rain and the thunder of
hoofbeats together in the seam of the horizon. Pale flame
tongues where white lightning meets the barren branches and
the thirsty weeds. Everything is about death, everything,
every waking thing, every dream.

Gauntlet

after *Gangs and Roses*, by Sebastian Domino (USA) contemporary

In transit, the rancid, fusty sweat of teenage testosterone. An involuntary heave, as the vehicle lumbers through the daily endless maze of concrete and steel. Heather grips two poles, her cane akimbo, and a searing poker rips through her damaged hip from the jolt and rumble.

She fixes her eyes bitterly on the smug maquillage of the princess in the blue-marked seat set aside for cripples, willing her to offer her space. The creature raises her eyes, then turns back to her texting with a huff. Now a stinking brute with the crack of his hairy ass exposed and his pants around his knees puts a size 16 sneaker onto her rheumatoid foot. She yelps and the sound is strange and animal.

She should never have left the house.

At the hospital, more poking and prodding, more violence from nice nurses with needles trying to find a way into her thin veins. She bears it all with all she can muster, and then the bruising thrusts against her ribs as a brand new technician fulfills his practicum taking pictures of her heart. Thank you, she rasps, shuffling out. Her leg is screaming down the corridor, to the lab. More digging in the desert of her fragile blood vessels.

Okay. Head home. The elevator is jam packed, as humid as the train back north will be. But she's okay. The corporate suits are always civilized enough to give up the blue seats, so she'll have a reprieve if no one steps on her. So long as she doesn't slip in the excrement landmines littering the trail from the hospital to the subway station.

Almost there. Hobbling. The sky is close and thick, threatening to break. She'll welcome that cleansing rain. Heather hears a metallic wailing start up behind her. *Go faster,* it says. *Walk faster!* She turns. The site of the damage on her hip is wailing too. One of the tent dwellers from the side street behind the hospital is teetering behind her, waving a filthy hand. *Get out of my way, lady,* he screams. *Go faster.* There is a crust of dried blood on his mouth and his eyes are wild. A tweaker. A wave of disgust moves through her when she smells him. The rank and ripe fluids of his rot. His teeth are erratic stubs in a cesspool when he opens his mouth to curse her.

She knows the route. The escalator down into the bowels of the train is a long one. She steps aside so he can go first, but he steps back and starts spitting and hurling expletives her way. She moves to the window and wall for stability. Go ahead, she says politely, as if nothing has happened. *Don't tell me what to do you fat cow!* the thing screams. *Get away from me!*

Away. She hasn't been anywhere else for a long time. It's nothing but pain and misery, mucus, edema, bruising. Every new throbbing pain gobbling up the life she once knew and taunting her with death. There was a time when she would have gone right up to the thing and given him what-for.

She'd always been fearless, until she was made vulnerable. Old. Thirty years prematurely.

She smiles nondescriptly. *Go ahead,* she says again, gesturing at the escalator. She can't go first. If he crowds her there, she might fall and break.

The thing is cawing and circling. Heather has nowhere to go. Then, out of nowhere, a white shirt appears and starts lambasting the tweaker. She is relieved, grateful, humiliated. She has always taken care of herself, even among the hardest of men, never had to leave her defense to kind strangers. But she sees her change and takes it, scurries as best she can to the escalator down into the train.

As she descends, she nods her thanks over the guardrail at the white knight come to her rescue, tears spilling. Sympathy flickers on his face. The tweaker is twitching with adrenaline but the knight is now the target of his hostility. He has forgotten about the slow-moving woman.

At the bottom, she hauls the heavy door open, escapes into a new crowd, and onto a crowded train. There's no room, but a much older woman with no devices sacrifices her seat. Heather is safe, at least, for now.

The Pillow Kings

after *Two Orange Cats*, by Louis Wain (England) before 1939

Mickey isn't sure why little boys in story books count sheep to fall asleep. He's never even seen one. He counts birds for Big Red, starlings, sparrows, wee chickadees. And grackles, too, especially those. There is an endless supply of those bully birds and he doesn't mind if Red eats all of them inside of his dreams.

In the morning, Big Red squishes himself onto the narrow window ledge and gives the yard his full attention. Mickey enjoys the drama. Red moves his head methodically back and forth, or up and down, to keep his eye on every fluttering thing. Sometimes his whiskers quiver. Mickey loves the funny expressions Red makes, and the staccato mewl, when the birds land on a branch tantalizingly close to the glass.

But for all of his predatorial pretenses, Big Red is a big softie. His main priority is arranging himself comfortably on Mickey's pillows. Mickey calls it the pillow king game. When he wants to nap, the boy can signal the cat to a new pillow or a pillow pile with a gentle pat or just rubbing his little fingers together. Then the great ginger will climb and clamber through the tangled sheet valleys, his purring machine igniting into a veritable rumble of thunder. He drools, he meows, he kneads the mountain. He nestles into the pinnacle of pillows, waiting for Mickey to put his head down beside him. Mickey loves the happy, comforting sound of Red's motor. He likes to hold Red's paw in his own, fidgeting on his toe beans while he drifts off. When they play pillow king, Mickey does not have to count birds.

Every day, Mickey's mom takes him outside for some fresh air. They walk slowly around the block. Mickey looks for cardinals and chipmunks that he could bring back, in him mind, for Red. There are a lot of squirrels but those are too big for breakfast. They sometimes see other children, kids playing tag or kicking a soccer ball around. His friends might wave or come over to say hi, when prompted by their Dad or a kind nanny. But no one really knows what to say. For awhile, Mickey would invite them to his room to play Uno or a video game. But now he just plays Big Red's games. It's easier that way.

Mickey was lonely at first, and scared. He couldn't understand why he was so tired all day and why he had so many bruises all over his body. He hid them at first so he wouldn't worry his parents. But his Dad noticed them and asked if he had trouble with anyone at school. He answered honestly that he was falling a lot. A teacher called to talk about how he was falling asleep in school. Then the doctor visits started, one after another. Needles, tests, tubes, and pills. He doesn't go to school anymore. He can do his lessons at home and someone comes to help him every week.

He isn't so lonely anymore, either. He is too tired most of the time to play anyways, and Big Red, his very best friend of all, is always there. He was scared when it all started, but now he has had a lot of practice in being brave. He barely cries at all now when the nurses run the needles through his arm or when he vomits. He loves his pillow kingdom. It is where he is most comfortable, where his arms and legs hurt the least. And if he does get sad or scared sometimes, Big Red always knows. He licks Mickey's ears with his scratchy tongue and makes him giggle. No one asks anymore what Mickey wants to be when he grows up, but Big Red knows. Mickey wants to be a cat.

Impossible

after *Northern Lights,* by Tom Thomson (Canada) 1917

And you know we gathered together and wept that night, that there was a bottomless glass for the bottomless well of our hearts when we heard you had stepped off of the world. It was cataclysmic, a latitude filled with swooping bats, a tectonic shift of the shapeshifting emerald northern lights we had once witnessed together. And, remember? That morning swarming with dizzy buzzy flies, how they were crawling out of the wallpaper and slivering slits of the wood logs, when we were at the cabin? All of these things premonitions now. How could it be? How was it that your long fine alligator feet and campy throaty laugh could be no longer? We were all there, circling the past and the future with fury and astonishment. There was just no way to take it in, this terrible, impossible thing.

The Surgeon

after *The Maldonado Mastectomy Exvoto,* by Unknown
Artist (Mexico) 1777

Hannah is glowing, he can tell already from the front door,
from the scent of spices and garlic, from the sounds of
sizzling and bubbling and funky jazz. Jamiroquai? It's been
a while.

Mike kicks off his work boots, grinning widely before he
gets to the kitchen. Hannah grins too and points to the faucet
when he reaches for her. First things first. "Who knows
where those hands have been," Hannah says, a bit of the old
her surfacing in her expression, as he scrubs the cars of the
day from his fingers. Mike sees that she has already
uncorked a nice bottle of Malbec to aerate.

"Well, don't keep me hanging," he says, pulling her close.
"Good news, I'm assuming?"

Hannah had not been as anxious this year as she'd been for
previous follow ups and scans. Her team saw no reason for
concern, with all of her markers showing consistent
improvements and nothing worrisome. Still, recurrences
were common and it was natural to fear them. Every No
Evidence of Disease report was a landmark.

"All clear," Hannah nods. Mike scoops her into his arms. He
doesn't try to hide his relief, kissing her head and face. When
he pulls away, Hannah sees his cheeks are streaming tears.
His hands move over her apron for a friendly fumble of her

breasts. "Good girls," he says, squeezing both gently. They are soft now with late middle age, and underneath, one is smaller, uneven and missing a nipple. But they're there, and Hannah is here. He's caressing them and kissing her neck now. He can't help himself, the relief.

"What did Dr. Shahan say?" he asks.

"Not too much," Hannah replies. "She said right away that the scans were all good, asked if I had any concerns." Hannah smiles, remembering the moment the surgeon strode into the little room where she was waiting, shivering and exposed in a flimsy paper gown. The doctor put Hannah at ease right away, didn't make her squirm for the reassurance she was waiting for. Dr. Shahan was a world-respected oncology surgeon. She was a wonderful doctor, a straight shooter, smart, and warm. And gorgeous. Amazonian tall, and big curly hair. She wore curvy sweater dresses with sneakers.

Like every woman, Hannah hated all the appointments and the treatments. She associated most of the health care team with trauma and didn't care for their ways. She always felt like cattle. Or worse, like a good repeat customer. Go here, do this, stand here, poke, prod, click, clack. But she had had a little crush on Dr. Shahan. Something about the doctor's confidence and authority. And how she smelled like warm vanilla, like toasted marshmallows.

Of course Hannah understood that lots of people developed unexpected attraction for a therapist or doctor. When someone nurtures you or saves your life, it's a powerful aphrodisiac. In the days that she was as bald as he was, while she was hunched over the toilet, she used to joke to Mike not to be surprised if she ran away to Costa Rica with Dr. Shahan.

With his hands all over her, swaying in the kitchen, with a slow beat and husky voiced Prince now crooning from the playlist, she can't help but thinking of the old days when they used to make love in the kitchen. Make love anywhere, everywhere. Mike was a skilled mechanic. He was good with his hands. They still made love today, but it wasn't like it used to be. The forced early menopause from chemo and losing half her breast had been hard on her. She missed this part of herself. She missed Mike, too, even though he was nowhere but here.

Hannah is getting lost in the slow dance, in sultry memories. In the glimmering images in her mind of Dr. Shahan's latex hands pushing her gently this way and that, tugging her breasts. "Dr. Shahan looked fantastic," she whispers suddenly, a catch in her throat.

"Tell me," Mike says after awhile. "Describe what you see." She finds herself sliding down onto her knees, her hands spread wide stroking Mike's big belly, fumbling at his jeans. Her husband starts to groan.

In the back of her mind, she is aware of the untouched wine that they will pour after this. She can smell the paprika and fish and lemon, the bright, fertile scent of life, hear the stew bubbling over.

She thinks about how vulnerable her body was on the operating table. The feeling of fear, of trust and pain and letting go. Dr. Shahan teasing her flesh open, cutting in to her tender flesh with scalpel and lancet, taking the diseased part of her away, cutting her back into wholeness.

Banana Pudding

after *Old Women,* by Istvan Réti (Hungary) 1909

The cream cheese icing on the carrot cake is an inch deep. Margaret stands in front of the glass display, tempted. Mother's recipe was just as moist and gooey and she loved cake with tea. It would be wonderful to bring a slice for her. Or the whole cake, to share with the other seniors stuck on the ward, waiting to die. A sweet spot in their day.

She moves on, ignoring the glistening pistachio baklavas and cheerful choir of colourful cupcakes beckoning. Mother has been on baby food and broth now for months. Even the soft body of cake is too solid for her to swallow. Margaret wants to bring her something kinder than tasteless mush, but it will have to be a pudding. She points to a cup of banana pudding, asks for a few of them to go.

Dan is waiting outside to drive her to see Mother. She pauses for a few minutes to steel herself before leaving the car. Dan touches her hand reassuringly. She can't help but noticing the years on his fingers, written around his knuckles like trunk rings tell the story of a tree. How does it all go so fast?

Margaret had been crying all last night after yesterday's visit. It had been a difficult one. Mother's loneliness weighed heavily on her. Margaret felt her terrible isolation acutely. There were dozens of others around her all the time, but Mother's speech was so garbled after the stroke that no one had the patience to listen to her. Margaret could understand only when she leaned in close and tuned everything else out.

But she was used to her and had learned to interpret the sounds.

Mother could barely see the television that was always on and always blaring at high volume. She couldn't even retreat into her mystery novels. She couldn't hold a paperback in her hands even if she could still see the words. Dan and Margaret came to see her on both days of their weekend, but Mother got very upset when they left. Yesterday she had just arrived when Mother said, "You walk in and you can hardly wait to turn around and get out of here."

And what could Margaret say? It was true, of course. The place was like a horror movie, complete with skeletons and zombies and mummies, the near-dead swollen and distended, or oozing and rasping, limbs held together with bandages. The stench of feces permeated everything. It was grotesque.

Margaret had stayed much longer than she wanted yesterday, to show Mother she cared. She read her some old-fashioned poetry and brushed her hair and took her measurements so she could order a fresh round of nighties and underwear and jogging suits. Mother got angry when Margaret measured her for a new bra. "I'm a 36 D!" she had hollered, and Margaret had giggled involuntarily. "That was a few million years ago," she thought, while Mother slapped at the tape measure angrily, complaining that the new bra would be way too large for her. Margaret was spooning some apple sauce into her mouth when Mother said suddenly and coldly, "I want you to go now. It exhausts me to have to entertain you."

But here she was. Coming back for more. Dan told her plainly that the reason Mother had no other guests but them was Mother's own doing. And she knew it was true. But still she hurt for her.

As they get out of the elevator, Margaret sees Mother's wheelchair next to another white-haired woman, and it looks cozy. Her heart leaps inside, thinking Mom had found a friend. But when they get closer, when she puts a warm arm around Mother and squeezes, the other lady looks up at her and barks, "Oh, good. Can you get this woman away from me? She's bothering me."

Dan is still holding Mother's banana pudding. "How is she bothering you?" he asks gently. There are so many different ways that Mother can bother another.

"I don't care for her weird stare," the lady says. "It's giving me the creeps."

Mother's eyes are creepy, both wandering off in different directions and rolling about, unfocused, glassy. Margaret tries to reassure the other woman. "She can't help her stare," she explains. "She can't focus or see properly. It's brain damage from the stroke. She's just trying to see you."

The old woman is petulant and mean. "I don't want your excuses. Get her out of here."

"It's not an excuse." Margaret tries again. "It's a neurological fact."

"Nice try," the old bag battles back. "I know something about this. Because my daughter is a doctor."

Margaret hears herself even before she gives her thought her voice. She can't believe it, using a word she has probably never used once in her life. "And you're an asshole!" Margaret exclaims, louder than she usually talks if not quite yelling. Mother was a lot of things, yes, but she couldn't help the damage to her eyes. Dan looks at her sharply, startled, then, amused. "Did you just call a 94-year-old lady an asshole?" he whispers.

Margaret looks down, then over at the lady whose smug expression makes her blood boil. She feels guilt immediately for losing her cool, wanting to apologize for being childish and rude to an elder. But she doesn't.

She pats Mother reassuringly, then sees Mother's expression, surprised and proud, pleased as punch, knowing Margaret went to bat for her, stood for her defense. It is fleeting, yes, but it's there. And it's the most Margaret has been given in years.

Ugly Crying

after *Christina's World,* by Andrew Wyeth (USA) 1948

He came in after work with an armload of sunflowers, yellow happy things, only to find her hunched on the bathtub's edge, weeping.

"Honey?" Eric called tentatively.

For May, crying was a private thing, something she did in secret, if at all. Through several years of pain, fear, and financial desperation, she had done what needed to be done. White knuckled her misery.

May was the strongest person he knew.

But here she was, full on sobbing, tears streaming, strands of snot sticky across her hands and hair. He has never seen this but recognizes it immediately from a Facebook meme: *ugly crying.*

In this rare raw and vulnerable moment between them, he has never seen her look more beautiful.

Eric put the sunflowers in the bathroom sink and sat down on the toilet, putting his arms around his crumpled woman. He braced himself for more bad news. A recent biopsy was clear. Was there a mistake?

May cried for a long time. Eric unreeled some toilet tissue, wiped at her face and hands. "Tell me," he said.

There was a shoebox on the floor next to a heap of laundry and crumpled Kleenex and an empty black garbage bag. Eric wondered if it held some old photos or letters. May reached for it and when the lid spilled off, he saw her old shoes inside. Black stilettos. May hadn't worn them in years.

Another torrent of sobs.

Eric took the shoes out. Then he put them back in the box. The nuances of his sartorial knowledge were limited. They were sexy high heels. Pumps? He thought that was the right word. Unfussy, like May. No straps, ribbons, sparkles, or gewgaws. Just sky-high heels. She used to wear them with tight jeans and let the hair out of her ponytail when she did.

May wiped at her face again. "Sorry," she said. "I was sorting in the closet. Throwing out some of my old clothes. Making a pile for Value Village."

Eric nodded. "Okay, honey. What happened?"

May pointed to the pumps. "I realized these had to go."

Eric nodded. "Makes sense. They're no longer practical." He tried to connect the dots but wasn't computing.

May held up one shoe. It was shiny and pointy. She hiked up her yoga pants and tried pushing a swollen foot into the shoe. Since the Docetaxel last year, her feet were painful stuffed sausages and her ankles were almost the same circumference as her calves. The swelling had been much worse at the time, and had slowly reduced, but the oncologist said that for some people, the inflammation permanently damaged the blood vessels.

The iconic scene from Cinderella crossed Eric's mind, where the ugly stepsisters tried to wedge their feet into the glass slipper. Now Eric understood.

He gently took the shoe and put it back into the box, and pushed the box back into the discard pile.

"Honey, I love you," he said. "You're alive. I don't care about anything else." He put his hands around one of her puffy ankles and massaged it.

Even if the shoe might fit again someday, May's joints were a painful mess from the hormone blockers meant to starve new cancer cells before they could grow. It would hurt to wear them. The days for these shoes were indeed over.

"I care," May sniffled. How could she explain that losing your beauty was losing your power? She no longer felt like a woman. Her breasts had been amputated, reduced to ugly skid marks on her flat chest wall. Her ponytail, thick as a horse's, was a slimy clog somewhere in the shower pipes. Now she had wispy sad curls that barely covered her skull. Her most private places were thin and papery, and burned like fire ants if they tried to make love.

May knew she was lucky to have Eric, who would gladly go without, forever, just to be at her side. But she didn't want to live like sister and brother. When they were first married, they made love two or three times a day. Later, when things naturally tamed from the early heady rush, sex was still important to them.

Today, when she was going through the closet, and found the shoes, May remembered the time she'd greeted Eric at the door wearing nothing but the black high heels. He dove straight for her breasts with his hands and his mouth, dropping an armload of pink roses in the foyer. She can't stand the thought of his deprivation. Even if he had accepted it. Especially because he had.

She wanted to welcome him and reward him, not cringe in pain and cower in shame. What was life without life?

Eric sat there with May a while longer, her ankle in his hands. He felt unable to convey the depth of his love and relief that they had today, and maybe tomorrow, together. There were no words that could express it. It was much deeper than the jagged scars of her body. It wasn't the same primal, fleeting ecstasy he'd experienced in their heyday. It was much more than that, the way she had cheated death so they could continue to share their lives. Complete unity. It was profound and even, perhaps, divine.

"Honey? Eric? What is it, baby? Tell me." May took one of her soggy crumpled toilet tissues and wiped at the tears streaming over his stubble.

He kissed her, then stood up. Picked up the bouquet of sunflowers from the sink. "Let's get these beauties into some water," he said.

What else could he say? He wanted to spend the rest of his
life lifting her up, and nothing else mattered.

Bloom

after *Tree of Hope,* by Frida Kahlo (Mexico) 1946

The courtyard caught full sun in the late afternoons, when Rosa was desperate to soak up as much as she could. No one was ever in the garden at that time. Her body was exhausted from the school day, from the effort of sitting up straight in class and navigating the halls on her crutches. By the time she dragged her heavy limbs home, she liked to stretch out among the spilling sprawl of peonies and azaleas, to feel the elements against her skin.

Sometimes the touch of warmth and the vulnerable feeling of exposing her legs or midriff melded together in a different kind of heat. Rosa would wait for the bloom to come over her, quieting herself to perfect stillness, tilting her head back a bit, and concentrating on the secret spots of her body. When the feeling came, she let it meander over and through her, river fingers from the sky and earth moving right into the centre of her. She imagined slipping her shawl and blouse away and freeing her tender nipples to the touch of the sun. She imagined living without pain, unfurling herself with abandon, opening to the world the way a dancer would.

Today, just coming down from her reverie, she saw the gardener under the arbor, almost obscured by the bougainvillea. He had a bag of peat moss in one hand and lopping shears in the other. The old man looked as startled as she was. Rosa felt an intense wave of something wild at her core. Manuel saw only a tenant sunning herself in their shared space. But for Rosa, it was much more. She had never revealed herself before. Only family and her doctors had ever seen her. She always guarded her body greedily, letting no eyes access the networks of crisscrossing cicatrices mapping her surface. She hated how they looked, even more than she hated her constant pain.

And now her threshold had been unexpectedly breached. Her heart was hammering against her ribs, trying to break free. *I am sorry to disturb you, Senorita,* Manuel said. She noticed his sweet lips and his soft silver curls. He bowed slightly in the way he always did, then hoisted the bag of peat into the wheelbarrow at the stone fence, back to work, business as usual. Rosa observed his awkward gait as if for the first time- one of his legs was slightly shorter than the other. She also saw the dark muscles of his chest and arms, near the long wound on his neck that had never faded. She imagined touching it under a canopy of night blooms, hearing his voice share its origin story. She could feel his arms surround her, scars to scars.

The Foal

after *Mare and Foal with Spring Blossoms,* by Maud Lewis
(Canada) 1965

The filly was a tender yellow crumb when she finally landed,
near small enough to fit into the widow's cupped palms. I
had wanted to stay up through the night with the mare, but
Jane said what a mother horse needed most was privacy and
darkness. She left the barn window ajar for the starlight and
stepped aside. And there in the morning, sure enough, was
the spindly thing I had waited since last year to meet.

She had a caramel coat and golden eyes. I named her Taffy.

For awhile, I had been cold and dizzy and covered in bruises
from just a few chores around the barn. Jane asked me to
carry some feed bags in from the truck, then told me I had
better see a doctor. She knew everything about animals,
including humans, so I did what she said. I told my folks how
I'd been feeling. Mother crumpled when the nurse said the
word "leukemia."

I asked to continue my time with the animals in between
treatments. The widow hired another set of hands and told
me to come and go at my own pace. There were goslings and
piglets and unruly fields of cornflowers, but the foal was my
heart and my hope. I groomed her and kept her water fresh
and sang to her when no one was listening. The foal was born
just a few days before I turned thirteen. The smallest miracle.

I stopped going to school and it wasn't long before my classmates no longer came over with books and balloons and homemade cookies. I had always preferred to spend time on my own, exploring the woods or reading, but it still hurt to hear their laughter on the soccer field across from the hospital. It hurt even more the way they stared, after my hair fell out. I never felt that way with my foal, or with the old farmer and her sheep and goats and horses.

I did everything they told me but still I got smaller. And everything hurt, even the sunlight on my skin. I didn't tell anyone what was going on in inside of me, how lonely it felt to know you were going to die when you were just a colt yourself. Or maybe for anyone, anytime. Mother held me when she soothed my fevers with a cool cloth but she would turn away whenever the tears came instead of sharing her sorrow with me, and this became a barrier of some kind between us.

One afternoon in the endless waiting rooms, I was leafing through an old gardening magazine from the stack, and came across a paragraph about how beautiful buttercups are really invasive weeds. The article said they were toxic to grazing cattle. An idea came to me then, something terrible and wonderful. I began to bring bunches of buttercups to the barn and feed them to Taffy along with hay and apples. I read how most horses would naturally avoid the plant's bitter taste. But my filly would nicker and nuzzle and slurp them right out of my hands.

I wasn't expecting the farmer to find me in the field that afternoon, because when I left the barn she'd been busy fixing a tire on the tractor. But there she was, wading through the grasses in her Wellington boots, hands on her hips and fire in her face. I could feel her fury, but she sounded calm when she asked me what I was doing. I said I was picking wildflowers.

I could tell she knew I'd been feeding them to Taffy. "Those weeds aren't good for horses, child," Jane said. "In fact, they can be poisonous." She held out her hands, took the flowers, gave them back to the ground.

She wiped her hand on her overalls. "Never mind, child," she said. "You didn't know." But I knew she knew I did know. I felt a stabbing wave of guilt and panic, so intense that for a moment it was stronger than my fear. How could I explain the truth about my baby horse? I only wanted to take her with me.

Reluctant Saints

after *Kateri Tekakwitha* and *Santa Rosa of Lima* icons, by
Kathleen Sibilski (USA) contemporary

The girl was too young for *Beautiful Losers*, smuggled in
with a stack of dusty second-hand paperbacks someone else
had forgotten. The imagery was jolting, confusing, violent,
perverse. Yet, oh! How she wanted to be beautiful. And
tragic, too. All that poetry and pain welling up inside her
shattered parts like ecstasy. She followed Leonard Cohen to
Kateri Tekakwitha, the lily of the Mohawks, the maiden who
would become a saint. Kateri's pox-marked face turned
unmarred, they claimed, just after her early death. The girl
thought Kateri dark and perfect, with or without scars. She
uncannily resembled the forest friends the girl had made up
when she was small. When Leonard Cohen died, much later,
his leukemia-fractured spine was a garland of thorns. On that
day, the girl, now a middle-aged woman, was in Peru, at a
basilica, tossing crumpled psalms into the wishing well of
Santa Rosa of Lima. The patron saint of the indigenous
people of the Americas. The saint's skull a relic there,
blooming roses.

There's Something About Henri

after *The Medical Inspection,* by Henri de Toulouse-Lautrec (France) 1894

He wasn't really a count, at least not quite, but all the dancing girls called him that. At first only when his back was turned, but as time went on, with affection, in his presence, while they watched him paint the stories of Montmartre. And even when they took care of his most earthly needs.

He wouldn't become a count, either. He was far too fragile for hunting or horses. His bones were always breaking. Whatever was wrong with him was also wrong with a number of his cousins, including his stunted legs, which made up only a quarter of his short stature. It was something that ran in the family, the girls would tease him good naturedly. Everyone knew the bluebloods all married their cousins.

Henri came to them as empty handed as they came to the cabaret stage and the upstairs rooms. Though he had once stood to inherit his father's titles and wealth, he'd been cut off because Daddy didn't care for his painting. In his early days at the academy, they'd all been proud of his considerable talents, at how he could coax his brushes and daubs into masterly draughtsmanship, with perfect perspective and proportions. But Henri preferred to go his own way, working with loose, raw brushstrokes in a frenzied drama. And he liked to paint the people society ignored and shunned, the poor workers, the showgirls, the women who loved women. So they cut him off and cut him out.

Henri could be funny, bombastic, ornery, and tender, and Juliette was sweet on him no matter which of his mercurial moods were on display. "I don't know, there's something about him," she told her friend Marie as they waited in line for their medical check. The pox ran rampant among them and these inspections were routine, implemented by the state so they could remain registered to work in the upstairs rooms.

Marie agreed. She considered the little artist in his dandy bowler and monocle a good friend. Even with his terrible teeth and his brittle bones, he was attractive to her, too. "These women are alive," she had once overheard him telling a colleague in an argument about female purity. Though he had the same needs as the other men who frequented their establishments, Henri also enjoyed her conversation and took her work as an actress and model as seriously as he took any other profession.

Like Juliette, however, she was careful not to fall for him too deeply. He had been very supportive of their friend Suzanne, encouraging her painting talents. But after two years as her lover, he wouldn't marry her, and even her attempt on her own life didn't change his mind. Countless painters and quite a few of the girls were downright obsessed by the beautiful tempest of Suzanne Valadon, but Henri refused to enmesh any of his lovers too tightly. He said that no matter their feelings for him, they would end up mocked on account of his deformities in the world outside of this one.

Both friends were cleared, to their relief, for tonight's party. The Count would of course be the guest star, with his easel set up for work and all the decadent cocktails and recipes he enjoyed on the menu. He was a man of many robust appetites. He had actually invented the favourite beverage of the frequenters, aptly called the Earthquake, half absinthe, half cognac, and full guarantee that anyone who drank it would be out of their minds.

"Dance with me, Henri," Juliette pleaded later that night. She had already entertained a handful of travelling merchants with a penchant for red hair and long legs, and she was ready now for her own pleasures.

The Count harumphed gruffly, waved his stubby fingers towards a canvas in progress. She saw her own face materializing there, soft and hard simultaneously under a mess of copper tendrils. It was something to see oneself seen this way, immortalized in the beauty that she knew already was all too fleeting.

In the periphery of her vision, Juliette saw Marie, across the room and sipping a drink, the telltale glower of jealousy in her expression. Juliette sighed. So be it. They both knew that Henri belonged to both of them, to all of them, and to no one.

"Oh, Henri, it's magnificent," she cooed. He told her that one of the guests had already made an offer, and he offered her, his subject, part of his commission, as he always did. She leaned down to him, closer, so that he could smell her amber perfume, and kissed him sensuously without concern for her lipstick. "Henri," she repeated. "Won't you ever love me?'

The little artist bristled. "My dear Juliette," he said, "I love you with all of my poor heart and you know it already. Here it is on canvas for all the world to see." Juliette smiled. She swayed a little now as another drink took effect, feeling the orchestra well up in her throat, in her thighs. She kissed him again, and then reluctantly retreated, letting him get back to his painting.

The Hummingbird

after *Emma Livry, Le Papillon,* sculpture by Jean-Auguste
Barre (France) 1861

"Death is the mother of beauty…"
Wallace Stevens, "Sunday Morning"

Her wings are flames. Her slippers are wings. Sylph, sprite,
angel, farfalla: butterfly. Emma Livry, dancer, love-child of
a dancer and a diplomat, protegee of the great Marie
Taglioni, the first sylphide to dance a whole ballet en pointe
toes. Marie choreographs *Le Papillon* just to watch Emma
fly. Sculptors try to pin her to the earth, but bisque and
bronze cannot hold her. She is pure *ballon*, airborne,
diaphanous, floating effortlessly above the world. One ballet
critic writes: *She skims over the ground, the water and the
flowers, apparently without touching them. Shims like
feather and falls like a snowflake.* The stage in these days is
illuminated by gaslit lanterns. Emma knows the risks and has
signed a waiver, refusing all fire retardants. Her tulle ignites
before our eyes. She is swept off her feet, savagely burned,
her tutu melting into her flesh. For eight long months the
ballerina is in the prison of her bed, instead of flying.
Nineteen and dying, she still opposes dancers wearing safer
skirts. "Yes, they are, as you say, less dangerous, but should
I ever return to the stage, I would never think of wearing
them – they are so ugly." It is 1863. The hummingbird
succumbs to septicaemia. She is twenty years old. Sylph,

sprite, angel, farfalla: butterfly. Her slippers are wings. Her
wings are flames.

Wild Ride

after Ghost and Bones, by Jean Michel Basquiat (USA) 1981

I'd almost forgotten, the sun in your eyes. Driving west. We both wore mob wife sunglasses. Our own version of Thelma and Louise: with your thick fringe of black lashes and those ropes of surgical scars, you were Frida. I was Leonora. No peacocks, though, or monkeys, or sinewy black cats. We were travelling light. We were free falling. We drove past a choir of ghosts on the highway, falsetto sirens that beckoned us deeper into those woods and out of them. On and on. We rode the flatlands when the sun came up and kept on going.

The Suitcase

after *All Dressed Up With Nowhere to Go,* by Wes Coke
(USA) contemporary

The suitcase was a bright and cherry red, chosen to stand out
on the luggage carousel. It was otherwise an ordinary,
standard model, nondescript and serviceable for an ordinary
travelling man. Like a hundred such occasions before this
one, the man had retrieved his suitcase, hailed a taxi, and
unlocked another generic hotel room door. As he did every
time, he set his suitcase down on the faded carpet, peeled off
his derbies, socks, slacks, and tie. He immediately showered,
lathering away the redeye grime of airports and a sedentary
stretch of hours, seeking relief on his cramped muscles from
the heat and steam. He donned another generic white hotel
robe, poured a can of soda water from another little hotel
fridge.

After a few sips of his refreshment, Arthur slid his hands
over the familiar latches, eager for clean clothing. The latch
did not click open readily, and he fiddled with it in frustration
for a moment. Finally, he pulled his Swiss Army knife from
his keychain and worked at it with the little blade.

A heady fragrance rose up immediately upon opening the lid,
something powdery and sticky with flowers and vanilla. It
took Arthur a few seconds to register that the contents of the
suitcase were not familiar. Instead of his neatly folded brown
and blue apparel, there was a jumble of denim and satin,
tangled bijouterie, perfume bottles and other cosmetics

tumbling willy-nilly about. A dogeared slim volume of poetry. Sylvia Plath.

Arthur's hands were shaking as he took out the worn book and flipped through it. Who read poetry these days? *I am learning peacefulness, lying by myself quietly, as the light lies on these white walls…*

He put the book back down, momentarily closed the lid. Upon closer inspection, Arthur saw that it was the same suitcase, but not, in fact, his own suitcase. This one was somewhat scuffed, and its seams were faded. He'd already disposed of the tags outside the airport, hadn't even bothered to check them.

Reluctantly, Arthur put his slacks and shirt and tie back on, grimacing about putting his freshly scrubbed feet back into used socks. He hoped to find a change of clothes at one of the shops in the lobby. He called the airline to notify them of his mistake, hoping his own luggage was there and could be couriered to the hotel before his meeting tomorrow. He assumed they would send for the stranger's suitcase shortly. Thankfully, Arthur always carried his levodopa medications on his person, just in case something like this happened. For now, none of his colleagues knew that he lived with Parkinson's, and he preferred to keep it that way.

At the hotel bar downstairs, Arthur treated himself to a nice vintage red, a rare indulgence since his diagnosis, along with salmon pasta and a bowl of potato leek soup. While he sipped his Bordeaux, he wondered about the woman and the suitcase and wondered if she was sitting in another hotel bar, hoping to find her belongings soon. He looked around him, thinking it would be a wild coincidence if the woman was in this same hotel, awaiting word on her mobile phone.

Arthur retired to his room again after a quick stop to pick up fresh underwear, socks, and a pale blue shirt. They didn't have his pant size, so he'd have to make do with the ones he was wearing. He turned on the TV, sitting on the white sheets in his underwear and the white robe. The suitcase perfume still filled the room with exotic flowers.

When he grew bored with flipping channels, Arthur put the suitcase back on the table and opened it slowly, reaching first for the book of poetry. He pulled out a filmy camisole and trembled at the touch of the soft fabric. It was ivory with just a hint of jade, like parchment paper. He imagined the silky garment against the woman's perfumed skin. His pulse was racing. Taking her clothes out of the suitcase, touching her things, felt intimate somehow, like opening her secrets. How long had it been since he'd touched a woman's clothing? He couldn't remember.

He picked up a tube of makeup. Mascara, is that what it was called? No, this one was a lipstick. Something caught in Arthur's throat. He pulled the cap ends apart, saw an understated, sweet, apricot colour. He imagined how the cosmetic touched her lips, making them warm and supple and shiny. He put it down. After a while, he picked it up again. He brought it up to his mouth, held her lips against his briefly. A sad, strange excitement ran through him. Arthur couldn't make sense of what he was feeling. He stood there for a long time, holding the lipstick in one hand, the sensual, smooth fabric of the pale top clenched tightly in the other.

Finally, Arthur put the woman's belongings back into the suitcase, everything except *Ariel*. He took another sparkling water and swallowed his medications. Then be brushed his teeth. He started to read the poems. There were pencilled notes on some of the pages, and he felt like he was eavesdropping on another person's private thoughts. But he kept reading.

He couldn't stop thinking about the woman who owned the suitcase. He wondered about her name. Was it Emily? Olivia? Clair? He wondered, was she as lonely as he was?

The White Rooms

after *White Doors,* by Vilhelm Hammershoi (Denmark) 1899

Imagine, a labyrinth of corridors, white walls, heavy doors ajar one after another, Denmark's dreary beams angling in through the panes to cast grids of hoary light across the floorboards.

There have been dozens, maybe hundreds of paintings in this place. Ida never minds when he shifts a table from one side of the kitchen to the other or rearranges the scant array of objects in the rooms. Though they both abhor clutter and clatter, she never objects to the fact that their whole dwelling is his revolving studio; mobile, temporary stations with his easel and brushes and oily rags.

He is not interested in colour at all. He will put a bowl of apples behind him to avoid red and yellow. If he must use them at all, he desaturates the pigment until it is a feeble glow. The suggestion of a colour, at most. His peers sometimes suggest that his pictures are all ghosts. But white is not sterile and deserted. White is epic and intimate at once, a wild rainbow already. Milk, porcelain, linen, snow, are all different colours, after all. It is the subtle, luminous lattices spun from sun that he seeks, or the shifting of late morning into noon and the patterns reflected on the pristine walls.

The artist occasionally ventures beyond, into the frosty fields and the paths meandering through the woods that separate them from the neighbours. Even to the cities, Copenhagen, and abroad, London, Amsterdam, Paris. The artist paints all of that, too, stripping the noisy clatter of people and traffic from his cityscapes and concentrating on the lines and shadows of fences and architecture. His peers talk again, say he takes the heart out of a place before he paints it, leaving only the husk intact on the canvas. He disagrees. Silence has a soul.

Often, too, he paints Ida. She is again and again the dark figure in his rooms. Ida is timeless and beautiful in her upswept hair and her long black gowns. He seldom depicts her face in detail. It might give too much away. He does not wish for her strange spells to become the concern of the neighbours. He usually portrays her turned away, absorbed, dreamy. He paints her as if he is eavesdropping on her, looking in on her reading a letter or playing on the piano. He wants the swan curvature of her nape above the severe neckline, the suggestive softness of it.

Ida. When they were much younger, he painted her in the nude. He thinks back now on the jarring rouge of her hardened nipples as she shivered in the eternal cold, and how he bleached them to be more demure in the portrait. Perhaps his penchant for privacy wasn't so much about secrecy, but about mystery. Oh, how surprisingly uninhibited she was, how eagerly she shed her dresses and undergarments and assumed the poses. And now, though they were only fifty, he contemplated the truth that Ida would soon become the widow Hammershoi. He has been coughing up bloody sputum now for months, and the doctors found a spattering of stones in his throat, each of them already with tentacles reaching for the rest of him.

Ida will be fine in time, of course. Though they have been so used to each other, inseparable since their youth, she is as inclined to solitude as he is. She is the more pragmatic of them, also. They have shared their grief with one another already, often talking late into the night after going over the pertinent affairs. Ida is almost comfortable in her chin-up resignation. It is Vilhelm who is uneasy. He does not know how to go without her. And he would like a few more decades to paint these rooms and to walk outside under the slate sky of November, to find those exact shades, steel, smoke, clay, gull.

Sometimes when he wakes from coughing, from the pain, he rises and steps outside so that he won't trouble Ida. He stares up at the stars sprinkled throughout the shadows of the branches. On these nights, he sometimes thinks about an afternoon almost as long ago as painting Ida naked. He and his brother and other young men liked to drink wine and picnic in the clearing of these very woods when it was sunny. Full of wine and poetry and laughter, he had needed to relieve himself and maundered away into the woods to do so.

And there, tethered to the tree by a noose, a man swaying solemnly from a bough, slumped in a dark overcoat, a shiny row of black buttons on narrow white boots pointing oddly down like dead geese at the market. And how in that moment everything receded into the distance, all the thrumming,

teeming signals of life dialed way down. How the world fell
silent there, and so far away. How he never quite came back
to it at all.

Strange Fire

after *Viva La Vida,* by Frida Kahlo (Mexico) 1954

And finally, she is finished, and tells him so. In three decades, defeat was never once in her vocabulary, so he knows it is real. A dagger through his heart.

"My God, Palomita." He takes her hand, wraps her tiny frame in the mountain of him. "You must not give up. I cannot live without you!" He buries his face in the dark tangled cloak of her hair, inhaling masa and Shalimar.

"Diego, you have to." Frida's face is a dark river.

For as long as he has known her, he has understood the pain was too much for her. She defiantly proved him wrong every day. First, hunting him down and extricating him, ever so indelicately, from the arms of his wife and his mistress, to claim him. Then, nonchalantly dismissing her dream to become a doctor and choosing instead to document her body's terrible journey. She painted on her back towards the ceiling, in a body cast, until she had, in his own opinion, far surpassed him, the celebrated master artist of Mexico.

But no longer.

"I cannot bear it anymore, Frida confesses. "I've tried everything."

Together they walk to the garden. They both love to sit and smoke among the bougainvillea and jacaranda and oleander; among the ancient Mayan artifacts they've collected. She is wearing the colourful leather prosthetic she'd had made after the amputation of her leg last year. He steadies her with his arm, eases her onto a bench.

Frida has never been frail. His first recollection of her was pure feistiness. She was barely a teenager and he was in his thirties, already famous, working on a mural at her school. Her small body was damaged already then by spina bifuda and a harrowing round of polio, but she was fierce and independent. The usual anxieties and insecurities that defined other teenagers were absent in this magnificent child. She openly flirted, and wore her broken gait with confidence. She had an unusual dignity and self-assurance, and there was a strange fire in her eyes.*

When she asked to watch him work, of course he obliged. Years later, he met her again at a meeting for the revolution. She was in recovery from a trolley crash that had left her spine and pelvis in pieces. She brought him a portfolio of her paintings, and she also made her desires known. He was intensely attracted to her, but told her he was married, and had children with several other women abroad. Frida laughed and said of course she knew all about it. Everyone did. She had many lovers of her own, she'd added with a wink, including women.

Frida had said once she could not speak of Diego as her husband. "He never has been, nor will he ever be, anybody's husband."** But in a certain way, he had only ever belonged to her, to no one else. They had divorced once, many years ago, but neither of them could stand to be apart, and they'd married again a year later.

Seeing her suffer had long undone him. He had not been able to protect her from the cruel disintegration of the body. It had started before he knew her. With every new cut of the surgeon's scalpel, he himself was diminished. She lived in agony day in and day out, but even so, she had never been fragile. She worked on crutches, and from a wheelchair, when necessary. She travelled to show her work or accompany him on his. After they took her leg, she defied the doctor's orders and made a grand entrance at her first solo exhibition in Mexico City, with orderlies carrying her into the show on top of her bed, where she stayed for the party, dolled up like the queen she was born to be.

"Diego," she says after awhile, taking him from his reverie. She takes a flask from under her rebozo and draws a swig of mezcal. "Do you understand what I am telling you when I say I am finished?"

He studies her eyes. He sees how that fire has gone from them. There is a torment inside him so intense he can barely stand it. He can't help himself, weeping freely. But he nods.

"Oh, Panzon," she chides. "I can't bear to see you crying."

"When will you go?" he asks, to show her that he does, indeed, understand what she is saying. He has always understood her. They understand each other inside out.

"It is my birthday next week. I am getting ready now, and want to go afterwards. I will finish the watermelon painting I am working on."

He had already known her intentions, truth be told. The piece on her easel is so different from the others. A ripe, juicy arrangement of red and green melons. Here in Mexico, watermelons symbolize life. It is her signature swagger, this statement: *viva la vida*. Long live life.

"I have saved up plenty of morphine," she tells him. "But I will need you to take a pillow once I am asleep and make sure I do not wake up. Promise me."

Diego nods again. He is still weeping. "Okay, Palomita," he says. "We will talk with our friend the doctor. He will say on record that you have had a stroke."

He needs her to know that despite everything, he has never abandoned her, and will not now, when she needs him most. The hardest thing. But he must set her free.

Frida smiles. "Gracias, mi amor," she says, and buries her wet face against his big soft belly.

He does not know how he will survive this. So quietly that he can scarcely be heard over the twittering towhees and warblers, he sings to her, a lullaby.

**

*A line from *My Art, My Life: an Autobiography, by Diego Rivera* (Dover Publications, 1991, originally published by Citadel Press, 1960.

**A quote from *The Diary of Frida Kahlo,* Abrams Books, 2005.

Agony

after *Jesus Bound,* by Spanish Colonial School (Peru) 1800s

They were creepy at first, the churches. The opulent ornaments, floor to ceiling gold baubles and porcelain virgins, old ancient paintings of forgotten stories by forgotten masters. How everything shimmered into eternity, a thousand candles flicking flames across the heavy darkness.

And always, though, the gore. Rose could not wrap her mind around it. The crown of thorns pushed deep into bleeding eyeballs; the wounds of whip and spear spurting like a geyser. Rose's plaza shoebox church back home had a great sound system and spanking-new drums, but as far as art went, there was not even a stained-glass shepherd. The cross at the front was an understatement, just two intersecting pieces of wood. Adjusting to the intensity here was something else.

But soon enough, the grisly icons and frankincense clouds in lemony humidity became true sanctuary for Rose. There were a million museums and ruins and taquerias, there were mercados and cafes and cemeteries and silver. There were roadside buckets of pulque, and heaps of mangos and mameys. Rose went everywhere and did everything. But she kept winding her way back into the cathedrals. There was peace like a river in that glittery holy twilight inside.

Just a few weeks ago, Rose's oncologist freed her from the years of infusions and burns, told her frankly, *now's the time for something on your bucket list, and then we'll just work on making you comfortable. I'm sorry.*

Of course she'd known they were almost there. But you held out hope for a miracle or a misunderstanding.

All she'd wanted through these gruelling, tortured years was to go back to Mexico.

So she did. Just her and her little camera. She wanted to take a thousand photos, all that she would leave behind. The masks, the flowers, the shrines at the edges of the desert and the inner city. The glistening fatty meat on the grills. The salsa verde. The mariachi. The matadors and nuns.

Rose didn't tell anyone she met along the way that she was dying. Yet everyone in this weird and wonderful world could apparently see right through her and felt no obligation to politely ignore the matter.

A man at the taco truck had sharp, beady eyes and thick hands like boxing gloves. He pointed at the most fiery of the salsas and nodded, telling her in perfect English the chiles could erode aggressive tumors.

A beautiful young man with emo eyes at the next barstool, a DJ or dancer maybe, gestured to the server for a round of mezcal. He explained that mezcal was the tonic of Mayahuel, the ancient cactus goddess. It cured no one, but gave strength and sleep to those who were afraid.

At the flea market, Rose encountered the nephew. There was a cascade of plastic figurines. She reached for Cookie

Monster. *Cuanto?* The man wagged his finger. *You need something stronger for the troubles ahead,* he replied. He started rummaging under the table.

Rose smiled and waved him away. A nostalgic Sesame Street statue was all a girl could ask at the edge of this abyss, and she had a pocketful of pesos to make him happy.

But he shook his head. *You misunderstand me, senorita.*

This belonged to my aunt. She asked me to give it to someone like her. The man handed her a little devotional painting. It was a shockingly gruesome picture, with Christ crumbling under the thrashings of a brutal scourge. His back was a giant seeping wound.

My aunt found tremendous comfort in this reminder, the nephew said.

Rose shuddered, stunned. Reminder of what? she wondered. But she wanted it. Badly.

Cuanto? she asked again.

Nada, the nephew said and waved her away.

Rose stared at the little painting for a long time. She studied the beads of sweat and the scars and gashes and the fresh thrashes on Jesus' weary, flagellated body. She reached out and stroked the crudely painted Christ, tussled his halo, traced his brow, found her eyes welling with tears at the touch.

She had understood when the pastor warned that Catholics were obsessed with suffering. They were to eschew the violent imagery and abhorrent practices like trying to emulate the Lord's wounds.

But the empty, sanitized cross didn't say much either. What quantity of pain and degradation was appropriate to depict? Wasn't the gore more accurate?

And in a moment, with the unknown auntie's devotional art, Rose understood.

Tormenting ourselves with asceticism or pain was crazy and missed the point entirely. The very meaning of the incarnation. The agony was what made him fully human. To feel the screams of a woman giving birth, to suffer the isolation of a leper of patient with AIDS. Rose had always wondered why Jesus had to endure all that torture. Now she understood that it made him fully human. It was her pain, nothing more, nothing less.

Rose wept as she swept the Aunt's sacred painting into her purse. In that moment, she forgot that she was alone, impermanent. She felt connected to the Aunt, and to everyone, everyone with a sliver or a broken bone or a broken heart, or an unruly mass seeping from breast to brain and liver.

She placed the picture beside the bed when she returned to her room. Prayed for the courage to face the pain to come, the end of the physical realm. For the first time, she didn't look away from that reality or move it to the back of her mind. She contemplated the little painting, the river of blood and those wounds, the depth of its sorrow and truth.

And yesterday I saw you kissing tiny flowers
But all that lives is born to die

Robert Plant and Jimmy Page, "That's the Way"

Acknowledgements

With gratitude to the wonderful journals and anthologies
that first brought these stories to the world. (In order of
their appearance in this collection.)

Winter Light- *Heart of Flesh Journal*
Fiddleheads- *Dark Lit*
Snow Fall- *MacQueen's Quinterly*
Vore- *MacQueen's Quinterly*
Leaving- *Modern Literature*
The Place Behind the Orchards- *Blue Spinoza Review*
Flicker- *Ink Fish*
Frost- *MacQueen's Quinterly*
Shamrock- *MacQueen's Quinterly*
The Asylum for Idiots and Imbeciles- *Apple in the Dark*
Nerve- *Flash Boulevard*
Emma- *Ghost Parachute*
Southern Soul- *MacQueen's Quinterly*
The Desert Apothecary- *Emerge Literary Journal*
Uncle Satan: *Dancing About Architecture, and Other
Ekphrastic Maneuvers,* ed. by Cassandra Atherton and Oz
Hardwick, MadHat Press, 2024.
Vespertine- *Microfiction Mondays Magazine*
The Monday Jar- *Lothlorien*
Toilet Humour- *Flash Fiction Magazine*
The Man in the Golden Mask- *Wild Greens*
Sepsis- *Flash Boulevard*
Wasabi- *MacQueen's Quinterly*

Crow Funeral- *Stray Branch Journal*- longlisted in *Blank Spaces'* Sticks and Stones contest
The Manny- *Third Wednesday*
The Handlers- *Eclectica*
Sick Bed Blues- *MacQueen's Quinterly*
Gavage- *The Galway Review*
The Surgeon- *Brilliant Flash Fiction*
Bloom- *Hare's Paw Literary Journal*
The Foal- *Your Impossible Voice*
The White Rooms- *MacQueen's Quinterly*

cover design: Lorette C. Luzajic
cover art: *Study of Severed Limbs*, by Theodore Gericault (France) 1818